ANXIOUS ATTACHMENT RECOVERY SIMPLIFIED

The Ultimate Workbook to Break Free from
Fear of Rejection and Cultivate Strong,
Secure Relationships with Meaningful,
Loving Connections

ROCHELLE CLARK, LMT, CLT

ISBN
Paperback - 979-8-9992092-0-7
Hard Cover - 979-8999209214
eBook - 979-8999209252

Printed in the United States

Table of Contents

Introduction

Have you ever found yourself eagerly waiting for a text message that never comes? Your heart races, and your mind spins stories about what it might mean. Many people have experienced that gnawing anxiety in their relationships. It is the kind that might keep you up at night, wondering if you are truly loved and valued. This anxious attachment is where fear and insecurity can overshadow love and connection.

This book is designed to guide you on a journey of self-growth and transformation. It is written with an understanding of your struggle with anxious attachment, assisting you in making positive changes. You will uncover strategies to help you make the transition from anxious to secure attachment, and you will learn to replace fear with confidence and self-doubt with self-assurance. Fundamentally, this book will equip you with the information to create secure, fulfilling relationships. This process will not be instantaneous, but your dedication will lead to significant change.

Throughout this book, you will find journal prompts that encourage introspection and interactive exercises that will guide your hands-on practice. It also explores techniques for healthy emotional regulation, practices for self-compassion to nurture your sense of worth, and boundary-setting exercises to strengthen your relationships. I encourage you to engage actively with these exercises and content—the reward is emotional freedom and the capacity for lasting happiness.

Attachment theory is the foundational concept of this book. It explains how our early relationships shape our interactions as adults. If you identify with anxious attachment, you often fear abandonment. In this way, you might seek excessive reassurance or become preoccupied with your partner's actions. Here, you will learn about your specific triggers. You will gain insights into regulating your emotions, communicating effectively, and embracing self-worth.

My goal is to empower you to break free from fear and insecurity, instead creating meaningful connections with others and yourself. I am committed to translating complex psychological concepts into practical, accessible guidance. This book will be your resource for real, lasting change. Whether you are single or in a relationship, this book is designed for anyone who desires healthier, more fulfilling connections.

My experience with anxious attachment began years ago. I know what it feels like to question your worth and feel overcome with anxiety in a relationship. As a result, I created this book because I believe in the power of change. I have seen it in my own life and the lives of people close to me. My goal is to help you achieve the same level of emotional freedom and happiness.

Together, through this book, we will explore the depths of attachment and emerge stronger on the other side. This book is your adventure, your chance to rewrite the story of your relationships. Embrace the positive change that lies ahead.

1

Understanding Anxious Attachment

F rom our very first breath, the need to connect is woven into our human fabric. How we seek closeness, respond to love, and cope with emotional distance is shaped in the earliest moments of our lives. This chapter explores the enduring impact of these early attachments, focusing particularly on the anxious attachment style. Through an in-depth look at how attachment patterns are formed, how they manifest in adulthood, and how they shape relational behavior, this book explores why certain individuals experience relationships as both a source of comfort and a source of fear. By understanding the roots and realities of anxious attachment—and how it differs from other insecure styles—this chapter dismantles the emotional barriers that prevent us from experiencing safe, secure, and lasting intimacy.

Attachment Theory

Attachment theory was established during the 1950s by psychiatrist and psychoanalyst John Bowlby. He proposed that the bonds we form with our caregivers in early childhood shape the way we approach relationships for the rest of our lives (The Attachment Project 2020).

This concept emphasizes that a child's first experience of connection is with their caregiver, typically a parent (The Attachment Project 2020). If the caregiver consistently responds to the child's emotional and physical needs, the child learns that the world is safe, that their needs matter, and that people can be trusted (The Attachment Project 2020). This forms what is known as a secure attachment.

However, not all early bonds are secure. When caregivers are inconsistent—sometimes loving but other times inattentive or emotionally unavailable—the child receives mixed signals about whether their needs will be met. This confusion disrupts the formation of a stable attachment and can result in anxious-ambivalent attachment during childhood, which often evolves into anxious (or preoccupied) attachment in adulthood (The Attachment Project 2020).

In some cases, this inconsistency stems from a caregiver's own unresolved emotional needs. These caregivers may seek closeness with their child not to support the child but to fulfill their own emotional void. This often-unconscious dynamic can manifest as overprotection, intrusion, or using the child to validate their self-image as a good parent (The Attachment Project 2020). These patterns are frequently passed down through generations through learned behaviors.

Children raised in such unpredictable environments may grow up unsure of what to expect in relationships. They may internalize the belief that love is conditional or unstable and that they must work hard to earn care and attention. Over time, this creates a distorted view of how relationships function, marked by a heightened sensitivity to rejection and a persistent fear of abandonment (The Attachment Project 2020).

In this context, attachment styles represent different levels of ease with intimacy and separation, shaping how we form relationships and manage the complexities of human connection. Early attachment experiences serve as the blueprint for our social, emotional, and cognitive development, leaving a lasting imprint on our behaviors and interactions throughout adulthood (Copley 2024).

Types of Insecure Attachment

Within the spectrum of insecure attachment, three primary styles emerge—each shaped by early relational experiences and marked by distinct patterns of behavior and emotional expression (Copley 2024).

These attachment styles are not just behavioral tendencies; rather, they are deep-rooted responses to unmet emotional needs in early life, influencing how individuals engage with intimacy, connection, and vulnerability throughout their lives. Although this book's primary focus is on the anxious attachment style, it is important to acknowledge all three styles of insecure attachment for greater understanding. They include:

1. **Anxious-Preoccupied Attachment**

Often referred to as anxious-ambivalent in childhood, this style is characterized by an overwhelming need for reassurance, validation, and closeness. It commonly develops in response to inconsistent or emotionally unpredictable caregiving, where love and attention were intermittently given or withheld.

As children, individuals with this attachment style may exhibit clinginess and heightened emotional sensitivity, frequently seeking approval and fearing abandonment. For instance, a child might burst into tears every time their parent leaves the room, even briefly, unsure if or when they'll return with comfort or attention.

In adulthood, these tendencies often translate into dependency on partners for emotional security, an intense fear of rejection, and struggles with jealousy or possessiveness. For example, a woman in a relationship might constantly text her partner for reassurance, interpreting a delayed response as a sign of disinterest or abandonment.

2. **Avoidant-Dismissive Attachment**

This attachment style develops in response to emotionally distant or unavailable caregivers. Children in these environments learn to suppress their emotional needs and prioritize self-reliance as a protective strategy. This makes them appear unusually independent —for instance, a young child might fall off their bike and get injured but insist that they're fine, refusing comfort because they've learned not to expect it.

As adults, individuals with avoidant-dismissive attachment often maintain emotional distance in relationships, minimizing the importance of closeness and preferring autonomy over vulnerability. An example of this attachment style is if you are in a committed relationship but avoid discussing your feelings during emotionally charged conversations, brushing off concerns with "I don't want to talk about it."

3. **Fearful-Avoidant Attachment.**

Also known as disorganized attachment, this style blends elements of both anxious and avoidant patterns, resulting in an internal conflict between the desire for connection and the fear of emotional closeness. Often rooted in traumatic early experiences or highly inconsistent caregiving, fearful-avoidant individuals may crave intimacy but simultaneously fear vulnerability, betrayal, or being hurt.

In childhood, this can stem from environments that were both unsafe and emotionally chaotic. For example, a child might run to a parent for comfort after a nightmare, only to be met with anger or dismissal, leaving them confused and afraid of both isolation and closeness.

In adult relationships, these individuals may exhibit unpredictable behavior—swinging between emotional intensity and withdrawal—as they attempt to reconcile their conflicting needs for closeness and self-protection. Here, a partner might share deeply one moment and then disappear emotionally the next, afraid that their openness made them too exposed or unsafe. Trust becomes a fragile thread, and relationships often feel like emotional minefields (Copley 2024).

Anxious Attachment

Anxious attachment is a form of insecure bonding marked by an intense craving for emotional closeness. It provides a powerful perspective on the delicate interplay between desire and fear in our relationships. People with an anxious attachment style frequently face everyday triggers that can stir up feelings of insecurity, anxiety, and fear of being abandoned. These everyday triggers include:

- **Inconsistent Communication:** When partners send mixed signals or respond unpredictably, it can heighten anxiety. Delayed replies or sudden shifts in communication patterns are often perceived as warning signs of rejection or abandonment.
- **Perceived Rejection:** Feeling overlooked, dismissed, or emotionally sidelined can be deeply unsettling. Even subtle signs—such as a partner seeming distracted or uninterested—may be interpreted as a lack of care or connection.
- **Fear of Abandonment:** Any indication that a relationship might end—whether through breakups, threats of separation, or offhand comments—can provoke intense emotional responses rooted in fear of being left behind.
- **Lack of Reassurance:** Those with anxious attachment often crave consistent affirmation of their partner's love and commitment. A shortage of affectionate words,

gestures, or physical closeness can lead to growing insecurity.

- **Conflict and Arguments:** Disagreements, even minor ones, can feel threatening. There's often a fear that conflict signals the beginning of the end, making even routine relationship tensions emotionally overwhelming.
- **Jealousy and Comparisons:** Interactions between their partner and others—especially those perceived as potential romantic threats—can spark jealousy. Comparisons in terms of attention, appearance, or success can intensify feelings of inadequacy.
- **Emotional Unavailability:** When a partner struggles to open up or express emotions, it can leave the anxiously attached individual feeling unloved, unwanted, or emotionally shut out.
- **Physical Distance:** Separation due to travel, work, or long-distance relationships can escalate anxiety. The absence of physical closeness often fuels fears about the relationship's stability.
- **Ambiguity and Uncertainty:** Lack of clarity around relationship boundaries, labels, or future direction can be highly triggering. Uncertainty tends to amplify fears of instability and emotional loss (Copley 2024).

Cultural and Social Influences on Anxious Attachment

While anxious attachment is often understood through the lens of early childhood relationships, it's essential to recognize that these dynamics don't unfold in isolation—they are deeply shaped by the cultural and social environments in which we grow. Cultural norms dictate how emotions are expressed, how dependence or independence is valued, and what roles caregivers and children are expected to play.

For instance, in collectivist cultures where family interdependence is emphasized, emotional closeness and mutual reliance may be considered healthy and desirable. However, if emotional needs are inconsistently met or boundaries are blurred—such as when children are expected to care for the emotional well-being of parents—this interdependence can contribute to anxious attachment patterns (Strand et al. 2019).

In contrast, individualistic cultures like many in the West tend to idealize self-sufficiency, autonomy, and emotional restraint. In these environments, children who seek closeness, reassurance, or emotional expression may be viewed as overly dependent or dramatic, leading them to internalize shame around their emotional needs and potentially contributing to anxious attachment tendencies (Strand et al. 2019).

Social messages about love, worth, and success also influence attachment development. Media often romanticizes intense, all-consuming love, where jealousy is mistaken for passion and emotional turmoil for intimacy. These portrayals can reinforce unhealthy relational patterns and validate the anxiety-driven behaviors often associated with anxious attachment. Furthermore, societal pressures around gender roles can complicate attachment dynamics. For example, women may be socialized to be nurturing, emotionally expressive, and relationship-focused, while men may be encouraged to suppress vulnerability and prioritize independence. This mismatch can leave anxiously attached individuals—especially women—feeling emotionally unfulfilled in relationships with emotionally unavailable partners, perpetuating cycles of anxiety and insecurity (Marschall 2025).

Socioeconomic stressors also play a significant role. In families facing poverty, systemic oppression, or chronic stress, caregivers may be emotionally overwhelmed or absent, not out of neglect but due to survival demands. These conditions can create unpredictability in caregiving and contribute to anxious attachment development. Additionally, trauma and systemic inequality, such as racism, displacement, or generational trauma, can disrupt caregiving patterns and alter attachment development across communities.

Understanding the cultural and social contexts that shape attachment helps dismantle the myth that anxious attachment is simply a personal flaw or psychological weakness. Instead, it reflects a complex interplay between individual experience and broader systems, thus reminding us that healing is both personal and collective.

Recognizing Anxious Attachment in Adulthood

In romantic relationships, adults with an anxious attachment style often reenact unresolved attachment wounds from early life—patterns shaped by fear, emotional inconsistency, and unmet needs. These individuals tend to experience an ongoing sense of emotional urgency and a deep hunger for connection, driven by an intense fear of separation or distance (Copley 2023).

This fear frequently manifests in behaviors such as excessive texting, persistent need for reassurance, and heightened anxiety during physical or emotional absence. Even a delayed response from a partner can spark catastrophic thinking, triggering internal spirals of insecurity and fear of abandonment, even when there is no real threat (The Attachment Project 2020).

At the heart of anxious attachment lies a struggle with emotional vulnerability, trust, and intimacy. While they yearn for closeness, those with this attachment style often find it difficult to fully open up due to deep-seated fears of betrayal or rejection. This paradox—longing for intimacy while fearing the pain it might bring—can make emotional disclosure feel risky and overwhelming (Copley 2024).

Adults with an anxious attachment style also frequently grapple with low self-esteem, often placing their partner's needs and value above their own. They may internalize relationship problems, blame themselves for their partner's emotional distance or unavailability, and question their worth or lovability (The Attachment Project 2020).

This emotional landscape can lead to behaviors such as jealousy, clinginess, or a fear of being alone. While these reactions are often rooted in fear rather than intention to control, they can strain relationships and create a cycle of insecurity and emotional distance (Copley 2024).

Yet, it's important to recognize that these individuals also bring significant emotional strengths. They are often deeply empathetic, emotionally aware, and highly committed to their relationships. Their capacity for emotional attunement and connection can create deep bonds, provided they learn to balance their sensitivity with self-worth and emotional regulation (The Attachment Project 2020).

Attachment theory reveals that your earliest relational experiences shape the emotional patterns that you carry into adulthood, influencing how you connect, trust, and love. For those of us with an anxious attachment style, relationships can feel both deeply fulfilling and deeply frightening—marked by emotional intensity, a longing for reassurance, and a persistent fear of abandonment. Through an understanding of these patterns, you can take the first step toward change. And by recognizing the roots of anxious attachment and how it manifests in your adult relationships, you can begin to ensure greater self-awareness, emotional resilience, and healthier ways of relating. Though the imprint of early experiences runs deep, it is entirely possible for you to move toward more secure, balanced, and fulfilling connections with insight and support. The next chapter explores how you can begin practicing emotional regulation and mindfulness to enhance your relationships and connections.

2

Emotional Regulation and Mindfulness

E motions are a natural part of life—we all feel joy, sadness, anger, and everything in between, sometimes even on a daily basis. But sometimes, these emotions can become overwhelming, leading to reactions we don't fully understand or control. I still remember sitting on the cold bathroom floor after a particularly difficult breakup, my chest tight with frustration and guilt I couldn't name, feeling like I had no outlet. For some, intense feelings like these can trigger unhealthy coping mechanisms such as self-injury. This is where emotional regulation and mindfulness become essential. While many of us use coping strategies daily without thinking— like scrolling social media to distract ourselves or snapping at a loved one when stressed—not all of them are helpful. Learning to recognize, understand, and respond to emotions—rather than avoid or suppress them—can be life-changing. This chapter explores techniques like grounding exercises and cognitive reframing to build emotional balance, reduce distress, and create healthier relationships with yourself and others.

Emotional Regulation

Everyone experiences emotions—both positive and negative—on a daily basis. It is a normal part of being human. However, for some of us, these emotions can feel overwhelming, almost like riding a roller coaster that is out of control. Intense feelings such as sadness, guilt, frustration, anger, self-blame, or low self-esteem often arise before someone engages in self-injury. When emotions become too intense, there can be a powerful urge to do something—anything—that brings relief. In these moments, emotional regulation becomes a lifeline (Rolston and Lloyd-Richardson n.d.).

"Emotion regulation" refers to our ability to manage and respond to emotional experiences in effective ways. People use emotion regulation strategies—often without even realizing it—multiple times a day to get through difficult situations. Many of us rely on a range of coping methods and adjust them depending on what is happening around us. Some of these strategies are healthy and constructive, while others can be harmful (Rolston and Lloyd-Richardson n.d.).

Healthy coping techniques, like going for a walk to relieve stress, help to ease strong emotions and provide insight into what caused them. In contrast, self-injury is an unhealthy coping mechanism. Harmful strategies tend to cause lasting physical damage (such as scarring or chronic wounds), lead to unintended consequences (like deeper injuries than expected), or serve to avoid addressing deeper issues, like the way substances like drugs or alcohol are sometimes used. Self-injury, too, can be used as a distraction rather than a solution (Rolston and Lloyd-Richardson n.d.).

Here are examples of healthy emotional regulation strategies:

- Talking with friends
- Exercising
- Journaling
- Meditation
- Therapy
- Getting adequate sleep

- Paying attention to negative thoughts that occur before or after strong emotions
- Noticing when you need a break, and taking it (Rolston and Lloyd-Richardson n.d.)

And here are examples of unhealthy emotional regulation strategies:

- Abuse of alcohol or other substances
- Self-Injury
- Avoidance or withdrawal from difficult situations
- Physical or verbal aggression
- Excessive social media use, to the exclusion of other responsibilities (Rolston and Lloyd-Richardson n.d.)

Enhancing Emotional Regulation

Maintaining emotional balance creates a stable environment where your relationships and connections can flourish. This allows you to approach situations with clarity, reducing the likelihood of misunderstandings and conflicts. When your emotions are regulated, discussions become dialogues rather than debates, promoting trust and empathy between you and your partner. This stability promotes healthier interactions, where you and your partner both feel heard and valued.

Incorporating specific techniques into your everyday life will help you achieve emotional balance and regulation. There are several helpful techniques for learning how to manage and regulate your emotions:

- **Make space for a pause.** Emotions often come on suddenly—we don't usually decide to feel them. One moment we're calm, and the next, we're angry or upset. One of the most useful tools for emotional regulation is simply pausing. Take a deep breath and create a small gap between what triggered you and how you respond. I didn't always know how to pause. For years, my reactions felt automatic. I remember once snapping at a partner over something small, like forgetting to buy milk, only to realize much later it had nothing to do with groceries and more to do with feeling unheard. It wasn't until I started practicing this pause — literally closing my eyes and breathing before speaking — that I began to notice the emotions underneath. As such, this brief moment can make a significant difference.

- **Notice what you are feeling.** Becoming aware of your emotions starts with tuning into your body. Dr. Judson Brewer encourages curiosity about physical sensations— where are you feeling tension? Is your chest tight? Is your jaw clenched? Are your hands shaky or your stomach unsettled? These bodily signals can offer important insights into your emotional state. Focusing on physical sensations can also reduce the intensity of the emotion.

- **Identify and name the emotion.** Once you have noticed what you're feeling, try to put a name to it. Is it frustration, sadness, guilt, or fear? Often, we feel multiple emotions at once—don't be afraid to explore what might be layered beneath the surface. For example, anger might be masking fear or hurt. Naming emotions reduces their power over you, transforming them into manageable experiences.

- **Accept your emotions.** Instead of judging yourself for feeling a certain way, remind yourself that emotions are a natural part of being human. Feeling upset, anxious, or hurt doesn't make you weak; it makes you human. Practice self-compassion and remind yourself that it is okay to feel what you're feeling.

- **Act in line with your values.** According to psychologist Susan David, emotional agility involves noticing and accepting your emotions without letting them control you. Once you have acknowledged how you feel, you can choose your response based on what matters most to you—your values. This approach supports thoughtful, purposeful action rather than impulsive reactions, helping you build a life that reflects who you truly are (Klynn 2024).

Integrating these techniques into your life requires intention and consistency. Start by setting daily intentions for emotional balance. Each morning, take a moment to decide how you want to feel throughout the day. Use reminders, in the form of a sticky note on your computer or an alarm on your phone, to practice the techniques you have learned.

Interactive Exercise: Journaling

Create a simple journal entry at the end of each day. Note what emotions you experienced, what triggered them, and how you responded. Reflect on these entries weekly to identify patterns and areas for growth. Adding a gratitude component and recounting moments appreciated during your day can further enrich your emotional awareness.

Over time, this journaling practice might reveal surprising patterns for you, such as the way certain environments might trigger specific emotions. This understanding allows for strategic adjustments, such as seeking calmer environments when focusing on challenging tasks. This practice reinforces positive experiences and balances challenging ones.

Engaging in discussions about emotional regulation with your friends or family can create a support network that encourages mutual growth. Discussing challenges and successes can provide new perspectives, helping you and your loved ones refine these tools.

By integrating these techniques into your daily life, you will discover that emotional regulation transforms your relationship with yourself and those around you, enhancing connections rooted in understanding.

Mindfulness

Mindfulness means being fully present and attentive to what you are doing right now without getting distracted, judging yourself, or becoming overwhelmed by your thoughts and emotions. It is focused on noticing what is happening in the moment and staying grounded in it. This kind of awareness is developed through practices like meditation, which can help strengthen your ability to stay mindful throughout daily life. By training your mind to remain in the present, you can become better equipped to pause, breathe, and respond thoughtfully rather than reacting automatically—something especially useful during stressful or difficult times (Headspace 2023).

Techniques for Mindfulness Meditation

Mindfulness meditation techniques enhance emotional awareness, allowing you to notice your feelings without being swept away by them. This practice will help you reduce automatic anxious reactions by creating space between stimulus and response. This offers a moment to choose how you will react rather than being driven by habit. By exhibiting mindfulness, you will learn to observe your thoughts and emotions as they arise, gaining insight into their origins and effects.

Here is a list of popular mindfulness meditation techniques:

- **Focused Attention:** This is one of the most common meditation practices. You simply use your breath as an anchor for your attention. Focus on the rhythm of your breathing—like the rise and fall of your chest—and gently bring your focus back to the breath whenever your mind starts to wander.
- **Body Scan:** In this method, you bring awareness to different parts of your body, from head to toe. You might notice tension, sensations, or areas of discomfort, which can offer insight into how stress or anxiety might be showing up physically.

- **Noting:** This technique involves mentally labeling thoughts or feelings that distract you during meditation—for example, "thinking," "worrying," or "remembering." Noting helps you observe patterns without getting caught up in them, creating space between you and your reactions.
- **Loving-Kindness:** Instead of focusing on your breath, this practice centers around sending kind thoughts to yourself and others. You imagine different people—loved ones, strangers, even those you struggle with—and direct goodwill and compassion toward them. It's a great way to let go of negativity.
- **Skillful Compassion:** Similar to loving-kindness, this method asks you to focus on someone you care about and notice any feelings that arise in your heart. It encourages empathy and connection, which in turn can boost your own sense of happiness.
- **Visualization:** This technique involves bringing a familiar image, such as a loved one or a peaceful scene, into your mind to help you stay focused. Visual imagery can support calm and concentration, especially if sitting still is challenging.
- **Resting Awareness:** Here, the goal is not to focus on anything in particular. You simply let your mind be, allowing thoughts to come and go without getting involved in them. This is a more open, relaxed form of mindfulness.

Reflection: In this practice, you ask yourself a meaningful question like "What are you most grateful for?" and notice the emotional response it brings up, rather than trying to logically answer it. Using the question in second person ("What are *you* most grateful for?") helps bypass overthinking and allows you to tap into feeling (Headspace 2023).

One of my favorite techniques is the STOP technique. It is another mindfulness resource designed to help you pause and reset during your day, especially when things feel overwhelming as they often can. Even if you start your day with one of the mindful meditation techniques mentioned above, it is easy to slip back into stress or autopilot as responsibilities pile up. Practicing STOP throughout the day will help you reconnect with the present moment, become aware of your thoughts and feelings, and respond more intentionally to what's happening around you (Cognitive Behavioral Therapy Los Angeles n.d.).

The STOP method is a four-step approach that helps break automatic, reactive patterns of behavior. Each letter represents a step in the process:

- **S – Stop:** Pause whatever you are doing.
- **T – Take a Breath:** Breathe, focusing on your breath and grounding yourself in the moment.
- **O – Observe:** Notice what is going on—your thoughts, emotions, bodily sensations, and surroundings—without judgment.
- **P – Proceed Mindfully:** Continue with your day, choosing your next action with awareness and intention (Cognitive Behavioral Therapy Los Angeles n.d.).

By building in a moment of awareness, the STOP technique creates space to respond more thoughtfully rather than reacting out of habit. This mindful pause supports better decision-making, improves emotional regulation, and can lead to healthier relationships and greater overall well-being (Cognitive Behavioral Therapy Los Angeles n.d.).

Incorporating mindfulness into your daily life requires intention but offers significant benefits. Dedicating only five minutes each morning or evening to your mindfulness practice, you can create significant shifts in how you perceive and react to the world. It is natural for thoughts to drift during meditation, but remember to gently guide your focus back to the present when this happens, without self-criticism. Finding time for mindfulness amid a hectic schedule can also be challenging. Prioritize brief moments of mindfulness during routine activities like showering or commuting, turning these into opportunities for presence. For instance, each morning commute can be an opportunity for mindfulness practice. Instead of focusing on traffic frustrations, you might direct your attention to reflecting on your day or week, or simply by focusing on your breath.

By practicing mindfulness, you will create a foundation for emotional balance that supports healthier relationships and greater self-understanding. You will learn to overcome life's challenges with equanimity and compassion. The ripple effects of your enhanced mindfulness will also positively impact those around you, creating a community of greater emotional awareness and compassion.

Grounding Exercises: The Power of Presence

After experiencing trauma, it is common to deal with distressing symptoms like anxiety, flashbacks, or intrusive thoughts. Grounding techniques can be a helpful way to manage these responses by shifting your focus away from overwhelming thoughts or memories and bringing your attention back to the here and now (Schuldt n.d.).

The 5-4-3-2-1 technique is a prominent grounding exercise that uses your senses to anchor you in reality. Start by identifying five things you can see, four you can touch, three you can hear, two you can smell, and one you can taste. This method engages your senses, pulling you out of your mind's chaos and into the tangible world. Another technique is object-focus grounding. Choose an object nearby and examine it in detail—consider its shape, texture, color, and weight. This focus can distract from anxiety and provide a mental reset. Visualization techniques offer another path; imagine a peaceful place, perhaps a beach or forest, and immerse yourself in that scene with all its sensory details. You can expand these techniques with practice to include personal variations, such as noticing particular colors or sounds that offer personal comfort (Schuldt n.d.).

During a high-stakes team meeting a few years ago, I sat across from my overbearing boss, who had a knack for interrupting and undermining my ideas. As he began to critique my proposal mid-sentence, my palms grew sweaty, and I could feel my composure slipping. Instead of reacting defensively, I quietly anchored myself using the 5-4-3-2-1 grounding exercise. I looked for five things I could see (my green folder, my colleague's glasses, my notepad, the clock, and the window), four things I could touch (my pen, the chair, my bracelet, and the table edge), three things I could hear, two things I could smell, and one thing I could taste. Within seconds, my breath slowed. I calmly rephrased my point, holding eye contact and setting boundaries with grace. In that moment, mindfulness became a resource that helped me regain control, find clarity, and respond with confidence in the face of stress.

Personalization is central to making these exercises genuinely effective. Adapt them to fit your lifestyle and preferences for the best results. Choose sensory elements that resonate personally—maybe you are drawn to the sound of rain or the feel of soft fabric. Incorporating grounding into existing routines can also enhance effectiveness. Practice while commuting, waiting in line, or before bed. By weaving these exercises into daily life, they become second nature, allowing you to manage anxiety whenever it arises.

Grounding exercises remind us that presence is powerful. They provide a tangible way to disrupt anxious thought patterns and bring clarity to chaotic moments. Through practice, they transform into habits that enhance resilience and emotional balance.

Reframing Unhelpful Thoughts

Your thoughts shape your reality, influence your emotions, and guide your actions. Cognitive restructuring—also known as cognitive reframing—is a therapeutic technique that guides individuals in identifying, questioning, and changing negative or irrational thought patterns. It begins with understanding cognitive distortions—those misleading or exaggerated thoughts that cloud perception. Such distortions might include black-and-white thinking, overgeneralization, or catastrophizing. These patterns can amplify anxiety, making challenges feel insurmountable. Recognizing their presence is the first step toward change. By altering these ingrained thought patterns, you uncover the way to a more balanced emotional experience, allowing for more precise, more effective responses to life's hurdles (Stanborough 2023).

Cognitive Restructuring Strategies

Self-Monitoring

The first step in changing negative thought patterns is recognizing them. Cognitive restructuring starts with paying close attention to your thoughts, especially those that trigger distressing emotions or unhelpful behaviors. It is also important to notice when and where these thoughts arise. Certain environments or situations might make you more prone to distorted thinking. Identifying these can help you prepare ahead of time. For instance, if you're a student who tends to catastrophize during exams, your thoughts might spiral into something like: "I'm going to fail this test, fail the class, and fall behind everyone else." Becoming aware of this tendency lets you catch and challenge it before it escalates.

Journaling can be a helpful resource for this process. Writing down your thoughts, even if you're not sure what triggered them, can help you spot recurring patterns or distortions. With practice, you'll become quicker at noticing these unhelpful thought habits, allowing you to positively reframe them.

Gathering Evidence

Another central element of cognitive restructuring is collecting evidence to test your thoughts and beliefs. Start by observing what triggers emotional reactions—take note of who you were with, what you were doing, and how strong your response was. This can also include any memories or associations that were activated.

You can then weigh the facts that support or contradict a certain thought or belief. Because distorted thoughts can be deeply ingrained, replacing them requires a clear-eyed look at whether they're actually true. For example, if you tend to take things personally, you might often blame yourself unnecessarily. Looking at the facts may show that a situation wasn't about you at all.

Questioning Your Thoughts

An essential part of cognitive restructuring is learning to challenge your automatic thoughts, especially those that get in the way of living a healthy, balanced life. Using a method called Socratic questioning, you can examine how logical or biased a thought may be. Some helpful questions to ask include:

- Is this thought based on facts or feelings?
- What supports this thought? What contradicts it?
- How could I test this belief?
- What's the worst-case scenario? How would I cope with it?
- Could there be another way to view this situation?
- Is this truly black and white, or is there a middle ground?

If you often catastrophize, try listing multiple possible outcomes—not just the worst one—and consider how likely each is. For instance, before a public speaking event many years ago, I was convinced I'd blank out and embarrass myself. But after questioning that thought, asking myself – Have I prepared? Is that really likely? – I realized my fear wasn't grounded in fact, and I felt more in control.

Performing a Cost-Benefit Analysis

This involves looking at the pros and cons of holding on to a particular thought pattern.

Ask yourself:

- What do I gain by thinking this way?
- What does it cost me emotionally, mentally, or in relationships?
- Does it affect my job or personal life?
- What are the long-term impacts?

Seeing the benefits and drawbacks laid out can help you decide if it's worth changing the thought pattern. A good example of this is when comedian Hannah Gadsby decided to stop using self-depre-cating humor because the emotional toll outweighed the profes-sional gain. She recognized that while it had previously served as a tool for audience connection, it ultimately reinforced internalized shame and undermined her self-worth (Lyons 2018).

Generating Alternatives

Cognitive restructuring also involves creating more balanced, rational ways of interpreting events. For instance, say you didn't do well on a test. Instead of thinking, "I'm awful at this," you could reframe it as, "Maybe I need to try a different study approach," or "I'll look into ways to better manage test anxiety." Or, if your coworkers fall silent when you enter a room, rather than assuming they were gossiping about you, consider other explanations—maybe they were simply ending a conversation unrelated to you.

Another strategy is to create affirmations based on facts. An example would be, "I contribute positively at work," supported by actual achievements or feedback. This helps replace negative beliefs with constructive, reality-based alternatives (Stanborough 2023).

Interactive Exercise: Daily Thought Log

Create a dedicated section in your journal for a daily thought log. Record any negative thoughts throughout your day, noting the context and initial reaction. Then, challenge each thought by reframing it with a positive or neutral alternative. Reflect on this process weekly to track progress and identify areas for further growth. By extending your practice to consider personal reframing and societal or contextual perspectives, you deepen your under-standing and tolerance of the broader world.

Reframing negative thoughts embraces a balanced perspective. It acknowledges both strengths and areas for growth. It is about building an internal dialogue rooted in kindness rather than criticism, enhancing your potential. Remember that change takes time and practice. There will be setbacks along the way—moments where old patterns resurface, or progress feels slow—but each effort contributes to lasting change.

By consistently committing to this practice over time, you will be able to better manage anxiety and promote your resilience against life's uncertainties.

Inner Peace Practices: Breathwork

Breathing is extremely useful for managing stress, boosting mental clarity, and restoring a sense of balance in daily life. When done with intention, conscious breathing can significantly support your emotional and physical well-being. Here are just a few ways breathwork can make a difference:

- **Breathwork activates the body's relaxation response.** Intentional breathing techniques stimulate the parasympathetic nervous system—your body's natural "rest and digest" mode. This helps counteract the effects of stress by slowing your heart rate, lowering blood pressure, and reducing cortisol levels, promoting a state of calm.
- **Breathwork strengthens the mind-body connection.** Your breath is a direct link between your mind and body. By focusing on it, you shift your attention away from anxious thoughts and reconnect with the present moment, encouraging mental stillness and emotional clarity.
- **Breathwork helps regulate emotions.** Different breathing methods can influence how you feel—calming techniques like slow, deep breaths can reduce anxiety, while more vigorous practices (such as yogic *kapalabhati*) can increase alertness and energy.
- **Breathwork supports oxygenation and detoxification.** Deeper breathing draws more oxygen into the body, improving tissue and organ function. It also

aids in clearing out carbon dioxide and other toxins through full, slow exhales, supporting both physical vitality and cognitive performance.

- **Breathwork builds self-awareness.** By tuning into your breath, you become more aware of your physical and emotional state. This awareness helps you notice early signs of stress, giving you the chance to pause, reflect, and respond rather than react.
- **Breathwork is easy and accessible.** One of the best things about breathwork is how flexible it is—you can practice it anywhere, at any time, with no special tools required. Whether you're winding down at home or navigating a stressful moment at work, breathwork offers a simple way to reset and recharge (Body & Mind n.d.).

Additionally, here are three breathwork exercises that offer a practical starting point for reducing stress and promoting inner peace:

Deep Belly Breathing (Diaphragmatic Breathing)

This calming technique encourages deep, steady breathing from the diaphragm, helping to activate your body's relaxation response.

- Sit comfortably or lie down.
- Place one hand on your chest, the other on your belly.
- Inhale slowly through your nose, letting your belly rise.
- Exhale gently through your mouth, letting your belly fall.
- Focus on the movement of your breath and repeat for several cycles (Body & Mind n.d.).

Box Breathing (Four-Square Breathing)

Popular in high-pressure environments like the military, box breathing is a structured, calming technique you can use to regain focus and reduce stress.

- Sit upright and breathe in through your nose for four counts.
- Hold the breath for four counts.
- Exhale through your mouth for four counts.
- Pause and hold for another four counts.
- Repeat this cycle for several minutes, adjusting the pace as needed (Body & Mind n.d.).

4-7-8 Breathing (Relaxation Breath)

This technique promotes deep relaxation by lengthening and synchronizing your breath.

- Find a comfortable seated or lying position.
- Rest the tip of your tongue just behind your upper front teeth.
- Exhale fully through your mouth, making a gentle whooshing sound.
- Inhale quietly through your nose for a count of four.
- Hold your breath for a count of seven.
- Exhale through your mouth for a count of eight, making the same whooshing sound.
- Repeat the cycle three more times (Body & Mind n.d.).

Emotional regulation is about learning how to sit with your feelings, understand them, and respond in ways that align with your values and well-being. When emotions run high, especially in the wake of trauma or overwhelming experiences, it is easy to feel out of control. But developing skills like mindfulness, grounding, and cognitive reframing offers a path back to balance. These techniques help soothe emotional storms and build inner strength and resilience over time. The next chapter explores how building a strong sense of self through identity formation can deepen your emotional stability and personal growth.

3

Building Self-Worth and Independence

W e all face moments of self-doubt, disappointment, or pressure to meet others' expectations. In those times, it can be easy to turn inward with criticism or look outward for validation. But learning to support yourself from within—through self-compassion, positive affirmations, and internal validation—can build a stronger, more stable sense of self. This chapter explores what it means to treat yourself with kindness, understand your emotions without judgment, and recognize your worth without needing constant approval from others. We will also look at how developing personal autonomy—making choices based on your values—can help you feel more confident and connected in your relationships. Through small, consistent practices, you can start building inner trust, emotional resilience, and a healthier relationship with yourself.

Self-Compassion

Self-compassion is both a mindset and a measurable concept rooted in positive psychology, introduced by Associate Professor Dr. Kristin Neff. It consists of three core components: self-kindness, common humanity, and mindfulness. To practice self-compassion is to respond to our own pain and imperfections with care, acceptance, and warmth—especially in difficult or disappointing moments. It's similar to self-love, though less enduring, and distinct from self-esteem (Moore 2019).

The Pillars of Self-Compassion

Self-Kindness

This involves treating yourself gently when you're struggling. Instead of judging your flaws critically, approach yourself with patience and empathy. This means valuing yourself unconditionally, even when you feel like you may fall short. Examples include offering yourself care during hardship, being patient with your imperfections, and accepting your faults without harsh judgment (Moore 2019).

Common Humanity

Recognizing that suffering and imperfection are universal helps us feel more connected rather than isolated. We all experience setbacks, and embracing this shared humanity allows us to respond with compassion rather than self-pity. It's about seeing our struggles as part of the broader human experience and remembering that we're not alone in our feelings. This might involve reminding yourself that failure is a shared human experience and accepting your flaws as part of being human (Moore 2019).

Mindfulness

Mindfulness in the context of self-compassion means being aware of our emotions without becoming overwhelmed or ignoring them. It involves observing our thoughts and feelings with curiosity rather than judgment, staying balanced rather than reactive. This can look like staying calm during emotional distress, keeping perspective when things go wrong, or approaching sadness with openness (Moore 2019).

Building and Practicing Self-Compassion

Treat Yourself Like You Would a Friend

A helpful way to begin practicing self-compassion is to consider how you treat loved ones. While we can't always ease someone else's pain, we often validate their feelings and offer support. The same applies to ourselves (Moore 2019).

- **Allow yourself to be human.** Self-kindness and common humanity remind us that everyone makes mistakes—and that's okay. Instead of harsh self-judgment, try offering yourself the same understanding you would show a friend who's struggling. If you wouldn't see them as a failure for missing a call or making a mistake, why do it to yourself? Recognize that imperfection is part of being human.
- **Be as caring to yourself as you are to others.** If a friend were upset, you might comfort them physically or speak gently. Doing this for yourself—using soft words or kind gestures—activates your internal caregiving system, which can reduce stress and increase feelings of warmth and safety. Even small acts like using affectionate names or placing a hand on your heart can establish self-compassion, if done with sincerity (Moore 2019).

Build Self-Awareness

- **Notice your self-talk.** Rather than criticizing yourself for feeling bad, start by simply observing your inner dialogue. Replace negative statements like "I'm awful for feeling this way" with gentle affirmations such as "It's okay to feel upset." These "releasing statements" promote non-judgmental awareness and emotional balance.

- **Embrace self-acceptance.** Accepting both your strengths and perceived flaws allows you to see yourself more clearly. Self-compassion encourages you not to over-identify with negative thoughts or let them define who you are.
- **Practice mindfulness.** Mindfulness helps you stay grounded in the present without overreacting to thoughts and emotions. Practices like deep breathing, yoga, or guided meditations can be done anytime to restore calm and presence.
- **Challenge assumptions about yourself.** Let go of rigid self-beliefs like "I always get anxious in crowds." Give yourself room to grow and behave differently. Treat yourself with the same openness and flexibility you would offer a friend (Moore 2019).

Shift Your Perspective

- **Release the need for external approval.** Much of our inner criticism is rooted in societal expectations. For example, guilt overeating often stems from social ideals around body image. By detaching your self-worth from others' opinions, you will profoundly practice self-kindness.
- **Connect with others.** Talking with others about your struggles can reinforce a sense of shared humanity. Knowing you're not alone in your pain helps reframe challenges and strengthens your support system, boosting emotional resilience (Moore 2019).

Interactive Exercise: Responding to Situations with Self-Compassion

Start by recalling a recent situation where you felt you didn't handle something well—maybe you missed a deadline, said the wrong thing, or just had a rough day. Take a moment to notice how you spoke to yourself afterward. Was your inner voice supportive or critical? Now reframe that moment by asking: "What would I say to a friend in this same situation?" Write down a few of those responses. This helps shift your perspective and trains your mind to respond with more understanding.

Next, consider how many others have probably felt something similar. Instead of thinking, "Why is this happening to me?" try "This is something people go through." It's a quiet but powerful reminder that your struggles don't set you apart—they connect you to others. Jot down one or two thoughts that make you feel less alone in the experience, like "Everyone makes mistakes" or "Others have felt this too."

To wrap up, take one small, practical action to look after yourself. That could mean taking a short walk, giving yourself a break from a task, or simply saying, "That was hard, but I'm doing my best." The goal isn't to feel instantly better, but to practice responding to yourself with balance, care, and patience—just as you would for someone you respect.

Practicing self-compassion offers more than just short-term emotional comfort—it strengthens your ability to handle stress and recover from setbacks. When difficulties arise, a self-compassionate mindset helps you respond with understanding rather than criticism. This makes it easier to move forward, view mistakes as part of learning, and stay motivated without being overwhelmed by self-doubt.

Developing self-compassion takes intention, but the benefits are lasting. As you become more patient and supportive with yourself, you'll notice a shift in how you approach challenges and relate to others. This mindset encourages self-worth, emotional balance, and a greater sense of independence in your decisions and relationships.

At its core, self-compassion means offering yourself the same care and acceptance you give to others. It involves accepting imperfection and recognizing that growth comes from acknowledging both your strengths and limitations. With regular practice, self-compassion helps you face challenges with clarity and confidence, leading to a stronger and more balanced sense of self.

Affirmations: Words That Empower

Positive affirmations are widely used in psychology, mindfulness, and therapeutic practices because they can be highly effective when applied with intention. Research shows that people who engage in self-affirming activities are generally less defensive and more open to receiving feedback, even when it challenges their beliefs. Simply put, taking a few moments to reflect on your values and self-worth can strengthen your emotional resilience in the face of discomfort or criticism (Dole 2018).

I was first introduced to affirmations through cognitive behavioral therapy when ending an extremely stressful relationship. The affirmations became a central part of retraining my thinking patterns. For example, if I noticed myself getting anxious and upset, I'd visualize a stop sign and say, "I am safe. All is well." This helped break the cycle of anxiety and worry, steering my thoughts toward a calmer, more constructive direction. Since our inner dialogue is learned, it is also something we can reshape. Affirmations work by helping us shift our mental filters—choosing to seek out hope or possibility instead of confirming fear or failure (Dole 2018).

Creating Personal Affirmations

The more that affirmations reflect your voice and needs, the more effective they will be. Here are a few tips on how to create your own personalized affirmations:

- Use affirmations in the first person and present tense, with confidence—phrases like "I will recover" are more impactful than general statements like "Anyone can recover." The phrasing matters.
- Keep your language positive—focus on what you do want or believe, rather than what you are trying to avoid.

- Speak affirmations as if they are already true. This can feel unnatural at first, especially if you are still working toward believing them.
- If a statement feels too far from your current truth, adjust it to something more believable. For example, if "I love my body" doesn't resonate, try "I'm learning to accept my body." You can build up to the stronger version over time.
- Start with one or two affirmations and repeat them regularly—morning, afternoon, and night. Say them aloud, write them down, or repeat them mentally whenever negative self-talk creeps in (Dole 2018).

Incorporating affirmations into daily life amplifies their power. Consider starting your day with a morning affirmation ritual. As you brush your teeth or sip your coffee, repeat your affirmations aloud or silently in your mind. This sets a positive tone for the day ahead. Affirmation journaling is another effective practice. Dedicate a journal to writing down your affirmations daily, allowing you to reflect on them and track your growth over time. Affirmation apps, such as "I am – Daily Affirmations," are another solution to provide gentle daily prompts, keeping these positive messages at the forefront of your mind.

Overcoming Skepticism and Building Consistency

Skepticism about affirmations is not uncommon. Some might dismiss them as wishful thinking, questioning their tangible impact on self-perception. However, like any new habit, the key to success lies in patience and consistency. Encouraging perseverance is critical.

My close friend, Sarah, struggled with self-doubt for years but committed to daily affirmations. Over time, she noticed a shift in confidence and began pursuing opportunities she once deemed out of reach. To commit to affirmations, she started with simple exercises: Each night, she wrote down three affirmations and pinned them on her bathroom mirror. Observing this daily ritual reinforced the uplifting messages in her subconscious, shaping her day with optimism.

For those of you grappling with doubt, start small. Choose one or two affirmations that resonate profoundly and repeat them consistently for several weeks. Observe how they subtly influence your thoughts and behaviors. Embrace this practice with an open mind, recognizing that change often occurs incrementally rather than instantaneously. By integrating affirmations into your routine, you nurture a mindset that values positivity and resilience. These daily reminders of your inherent potential and strength enrich the journey toward building self-worth and independence.

Internal Versus External Validation

Validation means acknowledging that your feelings are legitimate and make sense. It comes in two forms: external and internal. External validation comes from outside sources, like praise, social media likes, or compliments. While it can be uplifting, its effects are temporary. Relying too much on it can leave you feeling empty or discouraged when the support isn't there.

Internal validation, on the other hand, involves recognizing and accepting your own feelings without judgment. It's a skill that takes practice but helps you become more emotionally grounded. Instead of depending on others to feel okay, you remind yourself that your emotions are valid, even if things aren't going well. This kind of self-validation supports resilience and encourages personal growth by helping you move forward with compassion and self-awareness (Foundations Asheville n.d.).

The Pitfalls of External Validation

Relying heavily on external validation can lead to two key issues. First, it creates a constant need for approval from others to feel good about yourself or even simply to be emotionally stable. Second, when that approval isn't given—whether through disapproval, criticism, or even indifference—it can trigger intense feelings like shame, anxiety, or anger, which often lead to unhealthy coping behaviors (Cikanavicius 2017).

For example, getting likes or positive feedback may temporarily boost your mood and self-worth, but the absence of that feedback can leave you feeling insecure, invisible, or rejected. You begin to tie your emotional state to how others respond to you, making your sense of self fragile and dependent on outside opinions (Cikanavicius 2017).

In response, some people become people-pleasers, prioritizing others' needs over their own and losing touch with who they are. They may struggle to identify their own values, thoughts, or preferences because they've been conditioned to focus on pleasing others. Others may react differently—by shutting people out, ignoring boundaries, or acting in self-centered ways to avoid feeling vulnerable. These behaviors can reflect deeper struggles with identity, self-worth, and emotional regulation (Cikanavicius 2017).

Strategies for Personal Acknowledgment

To enhance internal validation, begin by setting personal goals that reflect your values and aspirations. Focus on measuring success by personal growth rather than external benchmarks. This shift in perspective allows you to appreciate your efforts and achievements as meaningful in themselves, not just as stepping stones toward societal recognition. Regular self-reflection is important because it helps you understand what truly matters to you, providing you with clearer direction. You might engage in introspective practices like journaling or meditation to better understand your core beliefs and values. This will build a strong foundation for self-worth that remains steady despite external fluctuations.

It is essential to incorporate self-acknowledgment practices into your routine by recognizing and celebrating your achievements, no matter how small they may seem. Consider keeping a success journal where you document daily victories and milestones. This practice reinforces a positive self-image and reminds you of your capabilities. Celebrating small victories is also necessary as it establishes a habit of gratitude and appreciation for your efforts. Acknowledging these moments creates a sense of accomplishment and motivates further growth.

Remaining Resilient Against External Pressures

Shifting from external to internal validation can be difficult, especially when society places so much value on things like wealth, appearance, or status. These pressures can make it hard to trust your own judgment. But learning to handle criticism without taking it personally is an important part of the process. Look at feedback with a clear mind—take in what's helpful and let go of what's not. Building a strong sense of self helps reduce the emotional impact of other people's opinions.

It is also easy to fall into the trap of comparing yourself to others, especially when success is defined by external standards. But your journey is your own, and your worth isn't based on what others achieve. Focus on what matters to you—your values, goals, and growth. This mindset helps you make better decisions and stay true to yourself.

When you catch yourself wanting outside approval, pause and remember that real confidence comes from within. Internal validation means accepting who you are without needing praise or recognition. It means owning your strengths and learning from your flaws. As you practice this, you'll become less affected by others' opinions and more confident in your choices. Over time, it becomes easier to trust yourself, stay grounded, and build relationships from a place of authenticity and self-respect.

Personal Autonomy: Inner Freedom, Outer Peace

Autonomy arises from multiple sources, and a range of factors can influence how much freedom and control we experience in our lives.

Elements such as early life experiences, parenting approaches, and other aspects of childhood development can significantly shape a person's ability to act independently as they grow older. A key developmental theory highlights that children begin forming a sense of autonomy between eighteen months and three years old. During this stage, they start expressing preferences—choosing what clothes to wear, deciding which foods they like, and selecting toys on their own. When children are supported and given the space to make decisions, they're more likely to develop a healthy sense of independence. Conversely, those who are restricted or criticized for their choices may grow up with doubts about their abilities and struggle with self-reliance (Cherry 2025).

Several other factors influence autonomy:

- **Self-Awareness:** Understanding one's own emotions, desires, and needs is vital for making independent choices. People who are more self-aware tend to follow their inner motivations rather than external pressures.
- **Locus of Control:** This refers to whether someone believes they control their own fate. Those with a strong internal locus of control are more likely to believe their actions make a difference, creating a greater sense of autonomy.
- **Self-Efficacy:** Confidence in one's ability to succeed—known as self-efficacy—is closely linked to autonomous behavior. Believing in your own competence can increase the likelihood of acting independently.
- **Social Support:** Encouragement from family, friends, and communities can strengthen a person's ability to pursue goals based on internal motivation.
- **Freedom to Choose:** The degree of autonomy we experience is also tied to the actual freedom we have. People are more likely to feel autonomous when they can make choices without fear of judgment, coercion, or punishment (Cherry 2025).

Autonomy exists on a spectrum—some people are naturally more independent, while others may depend more on external input. A person's level of autonomy can also change based on their situation, shifting priorities, and life circumstances. While autonomy is a fundamental human need, its expression is shaped by cultural norms. In individualistic cultures, independence is highly valued, and personal goals, emotions, and desires are emphasized. In contrast, collectivist cultures tend to see autonomy as something that exists within a social context, valuing it not just for the individual but as a means to support and fulfill responsibilities to the group or community (Cherry 2025).

Strengthening Personal Autonomy

Our experiences during childhood and adolescence often shape how autonomous we feel, and there are several ways we can actively strengthen our autonomy in the present:

- **Strengthen self-efficacy.** Reflect on how confident you feel in handling different situations. If you struggle with feelings of inadequacy, look for strategies that help boost your sense of competence. This could include using positive affirmations or connecting with mentors who offer guidance and encouragement.
- **Develop new skills.** Gaining new knowledge and improving your abilities can increase your confidence and sense of competence. As you grow more assured in your skills, you're more likely to take initiative and act independently.
- **Acknowledge your value.** Believing in your own worth is central to autonomy. Support your self-esteem by practicing self-compassion and recognizing your strengths. When you believe your voice matters, you're more likely to make decisions aligned with your values.

- **Nurture supportive connections.** Surround yourself with people who encourage your independence. These individuals will motivate you to explore, provide help when needed, and celebrate your efforts and successes with you.
- **Embrace authenticity.** Autonomy is closely tied to living in alignment with your true self. Spend time understanding your core beliefs, values, passions, and preferences so that your actions reflect who you really are (Cherry 2025).

Independence Versus Interdependence in Relationships

Independence in relationships means preserving your own sense of self, including your personal interests, goals, and routines. It involves dedicating time to your passions, setting your own aspirations, and practicing self-care to support your well-being. Maintaining this individuality helps you stay whole and fulfilled within the relationship, allowing you to grow as a person and bring your unique strengths to the partnership. It also helps avoid the risk of becoming overly absorbed in the relationship and losing your identity (Mindful Health Solutions 2024).

Interdependence, by contrast, refers to a healthy mutual reliance between partners. It's built on open communication, shared dreams, and emotional support. Through collaboration and teamwork, interdependence nurtures closeness and trust, helping couples build a solid foundation that can weather external stress and challenges (Mindful Health Solutions 2024).

Creating a balance between independence and interdependence is important for both emotional well-being and relationship satisfaction. Holding onto your individuality encourages self-growth and prevents negative emotions like resentment or feeling trapped. At the same time, cultivating interdependence creates a deep, supportive bond, reinforcing a sense of emotional connection and belonging. This balance guarantees that both partners feel seen, heard, and valued, which is necessary for a fulfilling relationship (Mindful Health Solutions 2024).

Too much independence can lead to emotional distance, where partners feel detached or alone. On the flip side, too much interdependence can tip into codependency, where individuals rely too heavily on one another for emotional fulfillment. A healthy relationship exists somewhere in the middle, where both people can flourish together and as individuals (Mindful Health Solutions 2024).

Here are some ways you can balance independence and interdependence in your relationships:

- **Set healthy boundaries.** Boundaries help preserve both autonomy and connection. By clearly discussing and respecting each other's limits, you create a space where both partners feel secure, respected, and free to be themselves.
- **Have regular check-ins.** Make time to talk about how things are going in the relationship. These ongoing conversations allow both partners to share their feelings, identify any imbalances, and make adjustments as needed. They show a commitment to maintaining a healthy dynamic.
- **Practice flexibility and compromise.** Relationships require adaptability. Balancing independence and connection often means meeting in the middle and being open to change. When both partners are flexible and willing to compromise, it creates a fair and balanced relationship where both individuals feel supported and valued (Mindful Health Solutions 2024).

Building self-worth and independence are practices that are interconnected stepping stones toward a more fulfilled life. I remember the first time I said no to something I didn't have the capacity for—a weekend project I would've normally taken on just to prove my value. My voice shook, but I walked away feeling a little stronger. Maybe you've had a similar moment—where setting a boundary, though difficult, reminded you that your needs matter too. When we practice self-compassion, it can be as simple as forgiving ourselves for a rough day or reminding ourselves that mistakes don't define our worth. Affirmations might sound cheesy at first, but I've found that telling myself, "I'm doing my best, and that's enough" can shift how I show up in the world. Learning to validate ourselves before seeking approval from others takes patience, courage, and an open heart willing to embrace vulnerability. In the next chapter, this book will explore how these foundations of self-worth influence our ability to communicate effectively in relationships, an essential skill for promoting connection and understanding with those around us.

4

Effective Communication in Relationships

We all want to feel seen, heard, and understood in our relationships. But no matter how strong the bond, misunderstandings happen—especially when communication breaks down. Whether it is a small everyday disagreement or a deeper emotional rift, how we talk (and listen) to each other makes all the difference. Communication is about sharing feelings, values, and needs in a way that builds connection rather than tension. While it might sound simple, communicating clearly and kindly takes real effort. It means learning to listen without interrupting, expressing your needs without blame, and understanding that body language and tone matter just as much as the words themselves.

This chapter explores how communication acts as the foundation of healthy relationships. From practicing active listening to recognizing harmful patterns like sarcasm or stonewalling, you will find practical tools to help you communicate with more empathy, clarity, and care. Whether you are building new habits or untangling long-standing communication struggles, the goal is to create a space where both people feel safe, respected, and emotionally connected.

The Value of Communication in Relationships

Effective communication is a central element in any relationship. It is essential for ensuring a strong and healthy connection between partners. While every relationship experiences highs and lows, having a clear and respectful way of communicating helps overcome challenges and strengthens the bond (Better Health Channel n.d.).

At its core, communication is the exchange of information between people. In the context of relationships, it allows individuals to express their thoughts, emotions, and needs. Communicating effectively helps partners stay emotionally connected and guarantees that their needs are acknowledged and understood (Better Health Channel n.d.).

Practicing Clear Communication

Even in the most tight-knit relationships, mind-reading isn't possible. To prevent misunderstandings that could lead to frustration, hurt, or resentment, open and honest communication is essential. Each person communicates differently, so partners must find a communication style that works for them. Developing healthy communication habits takes time and effort, and it won't always be flawless (Better Health Channel n.d.).

To communicate clearly:

- Choose a time when you can talk without distractions.
- Think about what you want to say beforehand.
- Be direct and specific in expressing your needs and feelings.
- Use "I" statements like "I feel…" or "I need…" to take ownership of your emotions.
- Listen actively and empathetically to your partner's words and emotions.
- Share positive feedback—express admiration, appreciation, and affection.

- Be mindful of your tone and body language.
- Be open to compromise and recognize that agreeing to disagree is sometimes okay (Better Health Channel n.d.).

Non-Verbal Communication

Communication is not just about words. Instead, your facial expressions, gestures, posture, and tone of voice all convey messages. Non-verbal cues can sometimes carry more weight than spoken words. For instance, saying "I love you" with a flat tone may send a mixed message. It is important to ensure that your non-verbal signals align with your spoken message (Better Health Channel n.d.).

Listening Skills

Often, while someone is speaking, we are already thinking about what we want to say next. This can lead to missing parts of the conversation or overlooking important nonverbal signals from the speaker. Active listening is about fully focusing on both the words and the nonverbal messages being communicated. It involves understanding both the content of the message and the speaker's emotions and body language. To do this effectively, the listener must be fully engaged. It requires concentration, emotional awareness, and a genuine effort to connect. In fact, active listening is sometimes described as a tangible form of empathy (O'Bryan 2022).

Successful active listening includes three core elements:

1. **Listen for the full message.** Every message has two layers: the actual information and the emotion behind it. Active listeners pay attention to both what is said and how it's said, including body language and tone.
2. **Acknowledge the speaker's emotions.** When it's time to respond, focus on the emotional tone behind the message. Recognizing and reflecting these feelings helps the speaker feel truly heard and understood.

3. **Be aware of nonverbal signals.** Nonverbal cues—like facial expressions, gestures, voice tone, and speaking pace—can reveal more than words alone. Observing these details can provide deeper insight into the speaker's message (O'Bryan 2022).

Interactive Exercise: Enhancing Active Listening

Pair up with a friend or loved one for a role-playing exercise, taking turns playing the roles of speaker and listener. The speaker should narrate an experience, while the listener should focus on paraphrasing the speaker's main points and summarizing implied emotions. After the exercise, discuss the experience and highlight moments when active listening hit the mark.

Mastering active listening demands patience and practice. It is a commitment to offering another person your wholehearted presence and understanding. Active listening allows you to perceive both the words and underlying emotions and intentions of the speaker, creating relationships built upon trust and empathy.

Identifying Communication Problems

Before you can start improving how you communicate, it is important to first recognize the signs that something might be off. Here are some common indicators:

- **Passive-Aggressive Communication:** Passive-aggressive behavior shows up when someone expresses their frustration indirectly instead of addressing it openly. This might include making sarcastic remarks about your partner's habits (like always being late), giving them the cold shoulder as punishment, and making subtle digs about their choices. While these behaviors might give temporary relief, they don't solve anything and can build resentment over time.

- **Avoiding Conflict:** Pretending issues don't exist won't make them go away. Avoiding tough conversations only gives problems more time to grow and become harder to resolve later on.
- **Speaking Aggressively:** If your communication involves raised voices, blame, or dominating the conversation, it's a red flag. This kind of aggressive speech can create a toxic environment and push your partner away (Lamothe 2025).

Negative Communication Habits

Here are some habits that can damage communication and should be avoided when possible:

- **The Silent Treatment:** Going silent instead of speaking up might seem like you're setting a boundary, but unless you clearly communicate your needs, your partner may not even know something is wrong.
- **Rehashing the Past:** Bringing up old mistakes during every disagreement can feel like an attack and may stop real progress from happening. Focus on the current issue instead.
- **Yelling or Screaming:** Raising your voice doesn't make your point more valid—it often just intensifies the conflict and can harm your partner emotionally over time.
- **Shutting Down or Walking Away:** Leaving a conversation abruptly can make your partner feel abandoned and ignored. If you need a break, say so clearly and return to the conversation when you're ready.
- **Sarcasm and Insults:** Using humor to belittle your partner or take cheap shots only increases tension. If you're trying to ease the mood, keep it light and self-directed, not hurtful.
- **Disrespectful Body Language:** Non-verbal cues speak volumes. Avoid checking your phone, crossing your arms, or looking away when your partner is talking. These

behaviors can signal disinterest or disrespect (Lamothe 2025).

Enhancing Communication in Relationships

Clear and open communication is a skill that can be learned and improved. Some people may need encouragement and time to share openly, while others may express themselves more through actions than words (Better Health Channel n.d.).

Strategies for Healthier Communication

- **Manage your emotions first.** Before approaching your partner with a difficult topic, take a moment to cool off and sort through your emotions. Go for a walk, listen to music, or do something that helps you feel grounded. Starting the conversation from a calm state makes it easier to reach a resolution.
- **Choose the right time.** Timing can make a big difference. If something is bothering you, let your partner know you'd like to talk so they're prepared—not caught off guard. Giving a heads-up can reduce tension and help both of you approach the conversation more openly.
- **Use "I" statements.** Rather than pointing fingers, talk about how you feel. Saying "I feel hurt when you focus on work" is far more constructive than accusing them of "You never pay attention to me." This shift can lead to more understanding instead of defensiveness.
- **Prioritize listening and being heard.** Don't treat every conversation like a debate to win. Real communication means hearing your partner's perspective, even if you disagree. Make space for both voices to be heard and understood.
- **Focus on resolution and compromise.** The goal of communicating isn't to "win" but to understand each other better and find common ground. Whether you're

navigating hurt feelings or planning for the future, aim for mutual understanding and be open to compromise. That shared effort can help rebuild trust and strengthen your connection.

- **Establish clear boundaries.** Boundaries help prevent misunderstandings. For example, if money is a source of tension, you might set a rule that purchases over a certain amount must be discussed together.
- **Small gestures matter.** Leaving a simple note about where you're going or checking in during the day shows care and consideration. These small actions can help your partner feel secure and appreciated (Lamothe 2025).

Handling Difficult Conversations

Having a tough conversation isn't easy, especially the kind where the goal is to reach mutual understanding and agreement. These aren't your everyday chats like catching up after work, making weekend plans, or casually checking in. This is something more intentional—a conversation meant to bring unity. Sure, it might get uncomfortable or emotional, but when approached with love, patience, and a genuine desire to understand each other, it can lead to real connection and shared clarity (The Happy Marriage 2025).

Difficult conversations go much more smoothly when you prepare the right environment. Three key ingredients help: the right timing, enough emotional energy, and a caring mindset.

Timing Matters

Don't bring up a heavy topic when one of you is rushing out the door or when time is tight. If something has been weighing on you for weeks, don't expect to resolve it in fifteen minutes before bedtime. Make space. Go for a walk, grab coffee together, or settle into the couch with some snacks. Create a calm, distraction-free moment where you both have time to talk and listen.

Sometimes, you might not be ready to talk right away—and that's okay. If you need to sort through your thoughts or feelings first, say so. And if your partner needs the same, respect that too (The Happy Marriage 2025).

In the early days of our relationship, I always wanted to address things right away. My partner, on the other hand, needed time. He would sit with his thoughts before opening up, and that frustrated me at first. I process my emotions as I talk, while he prefers to reflect quietly first. Recognizing those differences changed everything for us. Now, I ask if we can set aside time to talk in a few days, and he no longer feels like he has to withdraw for days before we work through things. It's a win for both of us.

Think about how *you* process emotions—and how your partner does. Chances are, you're not the same, and that's completely normal. Use those differences to your advantage instead of letting them create friction (The Happy Marriage 2025).

Emotional Energy Counts

For a difficult conversation to be productive, both of you need to have the emotional capacity to handle it. If one or both of you are already drained—whether from work stress, lack of sleep, or just a long day—it is much easier to miscommunicate, take things personally, or lose patience (The Happy Marriage 2025).

Emotional energy is about being mentally and emotionally present. You need to have enough fuel in your emotional tank to be able to listen without defensiveness, speak without blame, and hold space for each other's feelings—even when they are hard to hear. If you are feeling off, it's okay to say, "I want to talk about this, but I don't think I'm in the right headspace right now. Can we find a better time?" Prioritizing emotional readiness helps keep the conversation grounded and respectful.

Come from a Place of Love

The most important ingredient in a hard conversation is love. When you are discussing something tender or complicated, it is easy to slip into blame or criticism. But remember, the issue is not your partner —the issue is the issue. And you are a team trying to work through it together (The Happy Marriage 2025).

Approach the conversation with kindness and compassion. Begin gently, with the intention to understand, not to "win." Be mindful of your tone, your body language, and the words you choose. Starting with empathy sets the tone for a safe and honest exchange. A loving approach means you are trying to get your point across, and you are also trying to protect the bond between you. You want your partner to leave the conversation feeling seen and valued, not attacked or shut down. Even if you don't resolve everything right away, the way you show up for the conversation can build trust and deepen connection (The Happy Marriage 2025).

You might say something like, "I'm bringing this up because I care about us and want us to feel close again," or "I know this might be hard to talk about, but I'm here and I'm listening." Small affirmations like that go a long way in reminding each other that love is the foundation, even in the tough moments.

Healthy communication is about showing up with honesty, empathy, and a willingness to grow together. It is learning to express your truth clearly while making space for your partner's perspective. When we listen to understand, speak with care, and approach even hard conversations with love, we create a foundation of trust and emotional safety. Over time, these everyday choices shape more resilient, connected, and fulfilling relationships.

As you continue building these skills, remember that the goal of communication is not to avoid conflict but rather to overcome it in ways that bring clarity, healing, and closeness.

The next chapter of this book will explore how setting and maintaining boundaries can further strengthen a loving connection by honoring both your needs and your partner's.

5

Setting Boundaries: Prioritizing Your Emotional Well-Being

We all have moments when we feel stretched too thin, overwhelmed by obligations, or unsure where others end and we begin. In these times, it is easy to lose sight of our own needs or feel guilty for wanting space. Setting personal boundaries is about protecting what matters most to you. Boundaries help you honor your energy, prioritize your well-being, and show up more fully in your relationships and responsibilities. This chapter explores how to identify your limits, communicate them clearly, stay grounded in your values, and set healthy boundaries in your relationships. By taking small, intentional steps, you can begin creating a life that feels more balanced, connected, and true to who you are.

Personal Boundary Setting

In today's fast-moving world, it is easy to fall into the trap of chasing the latest productivity hacks to stay ahead, but most of these short-cuts don't really work. Even before the pandemic, studies showed that many Americans were sleeping less to squeeze in more work, yet overall productivity continued to decline. Since the pandemic, stress, anxiety, and sleep problems have only gotten worse. We are more overworked, overstimulated, and disconnected than ever, with less free time and less physical activity (Sanok 2022).

The solution is right in front of us: boundaries. When we clearly define what we need to feel healthy and safe—and build routines or rules to protect those needs—it can dramatically improve both our personal and professional lives. Boundaries help us show up as our best selves in every area. They can be as simple as deciding how we want to be communicated with, setting limits around when we are available, or choosing which days are for work versus rest (Sanok 2022).

You might ask yourself, *So why is it so hard to set boundaries?* In a past unstable relationship, setting boundaries was initially deeply uncomfortable for me. Over time, it became easier, and my confidence grew. Similarly, someone who struggles with people-pleasing—often rooted in early life experiences—may fear setting boundaries because they associate self-worth with constantly giving. Ambitious individuals may see boundaries as signs of weakness. Others might see them as proof that they are not trying hard enough (Sanok 2022).

But no matter your background or past patterns, boundaries can be learned. I have seen people transform their relationships with work, time, and themselves through this process.

What Not to Do

Boundaries are about control—specifically, who has it. If you are not choosing how your time and energy are spent, someone else is. The mistake many people make is expecting others to change instead of taking action themselves. You might ask for more considerate communication, shorter work hours, or better flexibility, and feel let down when nothing changes. Eventually, you stop asking. You go along with what others expect, even if it drains you. But this only leads to frustration and burnout (Sanok 2022).

What to Do

The first step in setting boundaries is to shift your mindset. Boundaries are about choosing your limits and acting on them. You will not get everything you want, but it is important to make intentional choices that protect your energy and prioritize your emotional well-being.

Defining boundaries helps you recognize what is essential versus what is ideal. Start by separating your boundaries into two categories:

- **Hard Boundaries (Nonnegotiables):** These are firm lines you won't cross. For example, "I won't work with clients on Fridays."
- **Soft Boundaries (Goals or Preferences):** These are things you'd like to change, but they're more flexible. For example, "I'd like to start leaving work by 4:30 pm" (Sanok 2022).

Next, follow the steps below:

1. **Identify your top priorities.** Think about the one or two things you value most in your personal and professional life—things you can't live without. Maybe it's more time with family, or a job that doesn't sacrifice your health. Try this mental exercise: Imagine your current life isn't an option anymore—your job ends, your relationship changes, or you have to move. What would you miss most? What wouldn't you miss at all? What would you be excited or scared to lose? This will reveal your core priorities and also expose habits or situations that no longer serve you.
2. **Test one hard boundary.** Once you have identified a key priority, protect it with a hard boundary. Use what I call a "cutback experiment." Here, you will reduce or eliminate tasks and interactions that drain your energy and see what happens. For example, if you want to

preserve your energy at work to avoid burnout at home, say no to unproductive meetings. Replace them with quiet work time or simply end your workday at 5 pm, no exceptions. In your personal life, spend less time with people who deplete you and more with those who energize you.

3. **Practice a few soft boundaries.** Turn to your "wish list," things that would improve your life but aren't critical right now. For example: better sleep, less time online, or fewer emails. Choose soft boundaries that support these goals and test them out.

4. **Commit to what works.** After testing some boundaries, ask yourself: What worked? What didn't? What boundaries gave you the biggest boost in mood, energy, or focus? Choose one or two to stick with for the next quarter (Sanok 2022).

Interactive Exercise: Boundary Reflection

Take ten to fifteen minutes to reflect on your boundary setting. Write your responses to the following reflection questions in your journal:

- What improved after setting this boundary?
- What challenges came up?
- How do I feel now compared to when I started?
- What needs to shift to stay consistent?
- Which boundaries are non-negotiable? Which ones are still in progress?

By identifying patterns in these reflections, you can demarcate areas where boundaries require reinforcement to protect your emotional well-being.

Boundaries should be adaptable, evolving as we do. Regularly evaluate your boundaries, ensuring they align with personal growth and shifting interpersonal dynamics. This ongoing process guarantees your protective limits evolve to reflect who you are and where you stand in your life's narrative.

Setting these essential boundaries generates spaces conducive to emotional well-being and nurtures relationships founded on mutual respect and comprehension. These delimitations manage life's demands and preserve your sense of individuality.

Relationship Boundary Setting

In the early days of a previous relationship, my partner and I would often stumble into small misunderstandings—things like how much alone time we each needed or when it felt okay to switch off our phones. One evening, after yet another quiet disagreement, we finally talked honestly about what felt comfortable and what didn't. That conversation shifted everything. Boundaries, I learned, aren't about creating distance, but rather they're about creating clarity. They help both partners express their needs and limits with honesty and kindness, making room for mutual respect, trust, and deeper connection. Rather than avoiding conflict, boundaries help prevent the kind of unspoken tension that quietly builds into resentment.

Types of Boundaries in Relationships:

Physical boundaries protect your sense of safety and comfort, whether you're around strangers or loved ones. You might prefer a handshake over a hug or need to pause and rest during a long bike ride with a friend. You can also set limits around your personal space, like keeping others out of your bedroom or asking them not to clutter your workspace (Reid 2025).

Sexual boundaries relate to physical intimacy and communication around comfort and consent. Even in long-term relationships, it's important to regularly discuss preferences and reassess expectations around topics like frequency of sex and contraception (Reid 2025).

Emotional boundaries help safeguard your emotional health and guarantee others respect your mental space. This could mean asking someone to avoid certain topics during work hours or reminding yourself that you're not responsible for another person's emotional reaction, such as after turning someone down for a second date (Reid 2025).

Material and financial boundaries involve setting limits around your possessions, like money, clothes, or your car. If you're generous by nature, it can be difficult to say no, but unchecked generosity can lead to resentment. Clear boundaries might include saying, "You can use my charger, but please return it," or "I can't lend you money for new shoes" (Reid 2025).

Time boundaries help protect your schedule and energy. After a long week, you might skip a social event to recharge or agree to attend only for a short while. You could also ask friends not to call during work hours or postpone serious conversations with a partner until you're in a better headspace (Reid 2025).

Healthy boundaries in relationships play a central role in:

- Promoting independence and preventing codependency
- Establishing clear guidelines for interactions
- Establishing self-respect and a sense of personal power
- Protecting your physical and emotional well-being
- Defining each person's roles and responsibilities
- Differentiating your own desires, needs, thoughts, and emotions from those of others (Reid 2025)

Unhealthy Boundaries in Relationships

Many people struggle with boundaries because we're taught to take things at face value and assume good intentions. As a society, we are often more focused on maintaining peace than preparing ourselves for the possibility of being mistreated. Most of us don't expect others to exploit or harm us—until they do. Toxic relationships often reveal themselves when someone consistently pushes you past your emotional limits. These relationships are unstable, unpre- dictable, and filled with emotional insecurity (Hill 2018).

Building and maintaining relationships can be incredibly difficult. We expect connection to come naturally, but real relationships are complex. They involve emotional, behavioral, social, psychological, and even biological components that can make things messy. And if you're caught in a relationship with someone unstable, abusive, or toxic, leaving may be your only path to healing (Hill 2018).

Here are some common indicators that someone may be crossing or testing your boundaries:

- **Creating Psychological Urgency:** Some people use urgency as a manipulation tactic. They try to provoke a quick reaction by making you feel like something needs your immediate attention. It's a way of hijacking your decision-making process, pushing you to act on impulse. This tactic is common in both personal manipulation and marketing—where pressure is used to override your ability to think clearly or set boundaries.
- **Constant Efforts to "Lock You In":** If someone seems overly fixated on you, it might feel flattering at first, but it often means they see you as useful, not valuable. This is about control, not care. One example is a neighbor who constantly did favors for a young woman until she declined to help with something. Then, he became aggressive and vengeful. The kindness was a setup, not genuine regard.
- **Dismissal of Your Emotions:** People who manipulate or abuse often ignore your feelings. They use tactics like gaslighting—making you question your perception of reality—or stonewalling—refusing to engage, speak, or respond to you, leaving you confused and destabilized. These behaviors are about maintaining control by keeping you off-balance emotionally.
- **No Concern for Your Well-Being:** Someone with harmful intentions might ask you to lie, put yourself at risk, or make sacrifices they wouldn't make themselves. A toxic friend or family member may casually ask you to do

something that endangers your job, your safety, or your peace of mind, showing a total disregard for your welfare.

- **Forcing Unwanted Collaboration:** Certain people refuse to accept your "no." If someone repeatedly tries to rope you into their plans or projects despite your disinterest, it's a sign they're not respecting your autonomy. One professional shared how a colleague reacted abusively when he declined a partnership. That one refusal led to a campaign of sabotage and emotional distress that still affects him years later.

- **Disrespect for Your Privacy or Space:** Privacy is a basic human need. If someone consistently ignores your need for space, it signals a deep lack of respect for your boundaries. People who behave this way are often more focused on their own needs than on yours and are unwilling to consider what you are entitled to.

- **Subtle Erosion of Your Autonomy:** Manipulators often work slowly and persistently. They'll revisit the same request, conversation, or argument until you finally give in. This "wear down" strategy relies on repetition, exhaustion, and pressure to break your resolve. Over time, you may stop setting boundaries just to avoid the constant battle.

- **Entitlement:** Entitled individuals believe they deserve your time, energy, and resources without reciprocation. These relationships are rarely balanced. You will likely feel used, drained, and unappreciated, no matter how much you give. The dynamic is exploitative, not mutual.

- **Repeated Tests and Mind Games:** Testing boundaries can look like passive-aggressive behavior, stonewalling, or constantly ignoring your needs to see what you'll tolerate. These tests are not isolated incidents—they happen repeatedly, with the manipulator trying to gauge how much control they have over you.

- **Secretive or Deceptive Behavior:** Sneaky behavior often hides a deeper need for control. These individuals operate behind the scenes, withholding information, lying, or acting in ways that undermine your trust. Their secrecy is not about protection—it's about keeping power over you and your decisions.

- **Shifting Personalities:** While everyone goes through ups and downs, some individuals shift their moods, attitudes, and behaviors so dramatically and unpredictably that you never know what to expect. This unpredictability keeps you off-balance. It may look like emotional volatility, but often it's a tactic—whether conscious or not—to destabilize your boundaries and make you easier to manipulate.

- **Emotional and Psychological Manipulation:** Manipulators use a variety of tactics—gaslighting, lying, guilt-tripping, or even acting like the opposite of what they feel—to distort your sense of reality. These behaviors are designed to undermine your confidence and control your perception of yourself and the relationship. (Hill 2018).

Establishing Healthy Boundaries in Relationships

Here are some helpful strategies for establishing healthy boundaries:

1. **Reflect on your needs and limits.**

Start by evaluating your current situation. Ask yourself: What do I need? What am I not okay with? Keep your expectations realistic. Consider boundaries across different areas:

- **Physical:** Your personal space, noise levels, and daily routines
- **Emotional:** How emotions are expressed and managed
- **Mental:** Your thoughts, values, beliefs, and the information you take in (Relationships Australia n.d.)

2. **Acknowledge your responsibility to take action.**

In tough times, it is easy to fall into blaming others or feeling helpless. While some things may be beyond your control, shifting focus to what you can do empowers you. Instead of dwelling on what's wrong, look for ways you can respond constructively (Relationships Australia n.d.).

3. **Communicate boundaries clearly and respectfully.**

Let others know your boundaries in a calm and respectful manner. Use direct but polite language. For example, you could say, "I need to concentrate, so I'm going to close my door to avoid distractions." Being assertive and respectful helps others take your boundaries seriously (Relationships Australia n.d.).

4. **Follow through with action.**

If someone crosses a boundary, gently remind them of it and ask for their cooperation. If the behavior continues, think about what natural consequence you can enforce. For instance, "If I keep getting interrupted, I'll have to work later tonight instead of relaxing with you." Make sure to carry out the action you've outlined to maintain the boundary's effectiveness (Relationships Australia n.d.)

5. **Express appreciation when your boundaries are respected.**

When someone honors your boundary, take the time to acknowledge it. A simple thank you reinforces your boundary and encourages continued respect and consideration from others (Relationships Australia n.d.).

6. **Stay flexible.**

Boundaries aren't set in stone. Healthy ones allow room for adjustment depending on the situation. You have the power to uphold or relax them as needed—what matters most is that the decision remains yours (Relationships Australia n.d.).

Healthy boundaries are about knowing where you stand and choosing to protect that space with care and intention. They help you stay connected to yourself while remaining aware of the needs of others. When you set boundaries with kindness and consistency, you create the conditions for greater trust, respect, and authenticity in your life. Over time, these choices reduce stress and resentment and build deeper confidence in your own voice. In the next chapter, this book will emphasize how to heal your past traumas and emotional wounds, creating a brighter future for yourself.

Breaking Free

> *"Recognizing that you are not where you want to be is a starting point to begin changing your life."*
>
> Deborah Day

When you have an anxious attachment style, it's easy to feel like you're the only person who worries about their relationship this much. You look around at other relationships, and it seems like everyone is carefree and happy, able to enjoy everything good about their relationship without constantly worrying. But that's how you probably look from the outside too—it's only you, who's living with your fears and insecurities, and your partner, who knows your behaviors, who knows how you feel.

Research shows that around 20% of the population has an anxious attachment style, though (Moore 2023). Far more people are experiencing the same kind of insecurity than you realize—and many of them are desperate to break free from it. Having been through this myself and knowing that change is possible, I want to help as many people as I can who are going through the same thing. The change in my own life has been profound, and I've found a level of relationship security that I never imagined I'd get to experience.

I still remember what it feels like to feel anxious in every relationship in your life, though, and it's because of this that I wrote this book. I want other people to know that it's possible to break free, and I want to share the skills and approaches that helped me do it. I'd like to call on your empathy for other people with an anxious attachment style now and ask you to help me reach more of them. I know that sounds like a lot, but all you need to do is leave a short review.

By leaving a review of this book on Amazon, you'll help new readers find it and begin their journeys toward a more secure attachment style and a happier life.

Scan the QR code below to leave your review:

Remember, around 20% of people are living with an anxious attachment style, and they're looking for help. Together, we can make sure they find it.

Thank you so much for your support. It makes more of a difference than you realize.

6

Healing Past Traumas and Emotional and Psychological Wounds

You can't always see emotional or psychological trauma, but that doesn't mean it isn't there, quietly shaping the way someone thinks, feels, or moves through the world. I've learned that trauma doesn't always come from big, dramatic events. Sure, things like accidents or abuse can leave deep marks, but sometimes it's the quieter moments—a childhood where your needs were overlooked, the slow drip of chronic stress, or the loss of something that mattered deeply—that stay with you. What really defines trauma isn't the event itself, but how it leaves you feeling: unsafe, overwhelmed, or like the ground beneath you just isn't steady anymore. And those feelings can remain for a long time if we don't find space to acknowledge and heal them.

This chapter explores the many faces of trauma, its symptoms, and how it shapes our internal worlds. More importantly, this chapter also offers pathways to healing, reminding us that even in the aftermath of pain, recovery is not only possible but deeply personal. With the right support and tools, we can reclaim our sense of self, rebuild trust, and move forward with greater clarity and resilience.

Emotional and Psychological Trauma

Emotional and psychological trauma occurs when highly distressing events overwhelm your ability to cope, leaving you feeling unsafe, powerless, or deeply shaken. These experiences can cause lingering emotional pain, anxiety, or disturbing memories, and may leave you feeling emotionally numb, disconnected, or unable to trust others (Robinson, Smith, and Segal 2024).

Trauma doesn't always come from physical danger. While life-threatening situations often lead to trauma, any event that makes you feel isolated, helpless, or intensely overwhelmed can have a lasting impact. What matters most isn't the nature of the event, but how it affected you emotionally. The more frightened or powerless you feel during an experience, the more likely it is to leave a lasting mark (Robinson, Smith, and Segal 2024).

Trauma can come from a wide range of experiences, such as:

- Single incidents, like a car accident, physical assault, or unexpected injury, especially if experienced during childhood
- Chronic stress, including living in unsafe environments, enduring long-term illness, or repeated experiences of abuse, neglect, or bullying
- Less recognized causes, such as surgery in early childhood, the sudden loss of a loved one, a painful breakup, or experiences of cruelty, humiliation, or betrayal
- Indirect exposure, like watching disturbing news coverage or violent imagery online, that can also overwhelm the nervous system and lead to trauma, especially when seen repeatedly (Robinson, Smith, and Segal 2024)

Childhood Trauma and Its Long-Term Impact

Trauma during childhood is particularly damaging, as it disrupts a child's sense of stability and security. This can stem from:

- Unstable or unsafe living situations
- Parental separation
- Serious illnesses or medical interventions
- Abuse—physical, emotional, or sexual
- Neglect or exposure to domestic violence (Robinson, Smith, and Segal 2024).

Unresolved childhood trauma can leave deep emotional scars, making it harder to cope with stress in adulthood and increasing vulnerability to future trauma. However, healing is always possible, no matter how long ago the trauma occurred. With the right support, you can reconnect with others, rebuild trust, and regain emotional balance (Robinson, Smith, and Segal 2024).

Signs and Symptoms of Trauma

Everyone processes trauma differently, and your reactions—whatever they are—are valid. There is no "right" way to feel after a traumatic experience. Common emotional and physical symptoms include:

Emotional Symptoms

- Shock, disbelief, or denial
- Mood swings, irritability, or anger
- Anxiety, fear, or panic
- Guilt, shame, or self-blame
- Sadness, hopelessness, or withdrawal
- Feeling numb or disconnected (Robinson, Smith, and Segal 2024).

Physical Symptoms

- Difficulty sleeping or frequent nightmares
- Fatigue and low energy
- Trouble concentrating

- Rapid heartbeat or jumpiness
- Muscle tension, aches, or general discomfort (Robinson, Smith, and Segal 2024).

Healing from Trauma

For many people, symptoms of trauma ease with time and emotional processing. But reminders of the experience, like anniversaries or triggers, can bring back difficult emotions. If symptoms persist or worsen over time, it may be a sign of post-traumatic stress disorder (PTSD). PTSD happens when your nervous system remains stuck in a state of shock, and you're unable to fully process or move past the traumatic event. Regardless of whether the trauma involved death or direct physical harm, survivors often grieve the loss of their sense of safety and stability. Like any grief process, healing takes time and care. With support and healthy coping strategies, you can begin to move forward, reclaim your sense of peace, and reconnect with yourself and others (Robinson, Smith, and Segal 2024).

Move Your Body

Trauma can throw your body out of balance, leaving you stuck in a state of heightened alert and fear. Physical movement helps release built-up energy, burn off stress hormones like adrenaline, and support your nervous system in finding stability again. Aim to move your body for at least thirty minutes most days. If that feels like too much, three shorter sessions of ten minutes can work just as well. Choose activities that are rhythmic and involve both your upper and lower body, like walking, swimming, running, cycling, or dancing (Robinson, Smith, and Segal 2024).

Try adding mindfulness to your movement. Instead of distracting yourself, pay attention to how your body feels as you move. Tune in to the sensation of your feet hitting the ground, the rhythm of your breath, or the feeling of the air on your skin. I have found that activities like yoga, dancing, hiking, and swimming can be especially grounding because they invite you to be present in your body and fully engaged in the moment.

Stay Connected

After trauma, it's natural to want to withdraw—but isolation can deepen emotional pain. Staying connected with others in meaningful ways helps promote healing. You don't have to talk about what happened. Often, healing happens not through conversation about the trauma, but through simply feeling accepted, seen, and supported (Robinson, Smith, and Segal 2024).

Reach out. Find someone you trust—a friend, family member, therapist, or spiritual leader—who can listen with empathy and without judgment (Robinson, Smith, and Segal 2024).

Rejoin activities. Even if you don't feel like socializing, make the effort to engage in everyday routines with others. Doing normal things can help you feel more grounded (Robinson, Smith, and Segal 2024).

Reconnect with old relationships that have faded, or consider joining a support group for trauma survivors. Hearing others' stories can help you feel less alone and offer ideas for your own recovery journey. Volunteering is another great way to reconnect with your community and with your own sense of purpose and strength. Helping others can help restore a sense of control (Robinson, Smith, and Segal 2024).

Make new connections. If you're feeling isolated or far from familiar faces, explore opportunities to meet new people through classes, clubs, or local community groups. If socializing feels hard right now, try using vocal toning. Here, make humming or *mmm* sounds and adjust the pitch until you feel a vibration in your face. This can help your body feel safe and ready to engage (Robinson, Smith, and Segal 2024).

In the past, when I was struggling with a particularly traumatic ending to a relationship, I would frequently take walks and hum to myself. It was an effective way for me to feel completely present in my body and connected with the beautiful nature around me. Over time, it helped me feel grounded, present, and safe.

Regulate Your Nervous System

No matter how overwhelmed you feel, there are ways to help your body settle and find calm again. These self-regulation strategies can reduce trauma-related anxiety and give you back a sense of control:

- **Mindful Breathing:** Slow, conscious breathing can help reset your nervous system. Try taking sixty slow breaths, focusing especially on each exhale.
- **Sensory Tools:** Tune into sights, sounds, scents, or textures that soothe you. It might be the smell of lavender, the sound of music, or stroking a pet. Everyone responds differently—explore what works for you.
- **Grounding Techniques:** When you feel overwhelmed, bring yourself back to the present. Sit down and feel your feet on the ground. Notice your body against the chair. Look around and name six things you see that are red or blue. These simple actions can slow racing thoughts and help you feel steadier.
- **Feel Your Feelings:** Let your emotions surface without judgment. Acknowledging what you feel—instead of avoiding or suppressing it—is a vital part of healing (Robinson, Smith, and Segal 2024).

Support Your Physical Health

Your physical well-being is closely tied to your emotional recovery. Taking care of your body helps you better manage the stress of trauma. Here are ways you can achieve this:

- **Get consistent, quality sleep.** Trauma often disrupts sleep patterns, which in turn affects emotional resilience. Try to go to bed and wake up at the same time each day, aiming for seven to nine hours of sleep.
- **Limit alcohol and drugs.** Substances may seem to offer relief, but they often worsen symptoms like anxiety, depression, and disconnection. They can also interfere with quality sleep.
- **Eat to nourish your body and brain.** Fuel your body with regular, nutrient-dense, balanced meals. Focus on foods rich in omega-3s—like salmon, walnuts, and flaxseeds —to support brain health and mood. Avoid too much sugar, caffeine, or processed foods.
- **Manage stress.** Explore practices that soothe you— meditation, deep breathing, gentle yoga, or creative hobbies. Make time for joy and relaxation (Robinson, Smith, and Segal 2024).

Seek Professional Help

Healing from trauma is a process, and it is different for everyone. If you have been struggling for a long time or your symptoms are getting worse, it may be time to reach out for expert support.

Consider professional help if you are:

- Struggling to function at home, work, or in relationships
- Dealing with intense fear, anxiety, depression, or hopelessness
- Feeling emotionally numb or detached from others
- Haunted by intrusive memories, flashbacks, or nightmares
- Actively avoiding anything related to the trauma
- Using substances to cope (Robinson, Smith, and Segal 2024)

Trauma Therapies

Healing often requires more than willpower—it may involve therapy to safely process the trauma and release its hold on your nervous system. Examples of trauma therapy include:

- **Somatic Experiencing:** This method focuses on physical sensations to release trauma stored in the body. It helps discharge survival energy and restores balance through natural responses like shaking or crying.
- **Cognitive Behavioral Therapy (CBT):** CBT helps you reframe negative thoughts and beliefs connected to the traumatic experience, offering new perspectives and coping tools.
- **EMDR (Eye Movement Desensitization and Reprocessing):** EMDR uses rhythmic bilateral stimulation, like eye movements or tapping, to help unfreeze traumatic memories and integrate them in a healthier way (Robinson, Smith, and Segal 2024).

Treating Multiple or Complex Traumas

Narrative exposure therapy (NET) is a trauma-focused treatment designed for individuals who have experienced multiple or complex traumas. It is especially effective in community-based settings and has been widely used with people impacted by political, cultural, or social violence, such as refugees. NET can be delivered in small groups over four to ten sessions or provided individually. At the heart of NET is the understanding that the way someone interprets their life story shapes their perception of past events and overall well-being. When a person's life narrative becomes defined solely by trauma, it can lead to ongoing emotional distress. NET aims to shift this by helping individuals build a fuller, more balanced account of their lives (American Psychological Association 2025).

Treating PTSD

NET is a conditionally recommended treatment for PTSD. Guided by a therapist, the person constructs a chronological narrative of their life, focusing primarily on traumatic events while also including positive experiences. This process helps organize fragmented sensory, emotional, and cognitive memories into a coherent and meaningful story (American Psychological Association 2025).

Throughout the therapy, the therapist practices compassionate listening, establishes a strong therapeutic bond, and maintains a nonjudgmental, respectful approach. Patients are encouraged to revisit their trauma in detail—describing thoughts, feelings, bodily reactions, and sensory impressions—while remaining anchored in the present. This is done through reminders that the memories belong to the past and are linked to specific times and places. As the patient speaks, the fragmented memories are gradually processed and integrated (American Psychological Association 2025).

One unique feature of NET is that it does not require a person to isolate a single traumatic incident from many. Instead, it supports them in reflecting on their entire life, promoting a sense of identity and continuity. This helps clarify emotional responses and reveals how coping mechanisms and beliefs have formed over time (American Psychological Association 2025).

NET also stands out for its commitment to bearing witness to a person's experience. By documenting their life story—written by the therapist and presented at the end of treatment—NET validates the person's narrative, restores dignity, and affirms their human rights. For many, receiving this written autobiography provides motivation to complete therapy and serves as a powerful symbol of healing (American Psychological Association 2025).

Reflective Tool: Emotional Timeline Exercise

Draw up an emotional timeline, punctuating it with major life events and the emotions linked to them. This visualization will highlight the pathways between past traumas and current emotional states, offering a road map to understanding your emotional story. Recognizing these scars is not an invitation to wallow in self-pity, but rather a means of acceptance and acknowledgment of your past. It is about affirming to yourself, "Yes, this occurred. Yes, it was painful. And yes, it impacts me still." For many, this recognition proves transformative, providing solace and a release from trauma.

Inner Reflection: Gain Clarity on Your Inner World

Inner self-reflection is a realm for nonjudgmental observation and fearless exploration. Self-reflection extends beyond a cursory examination of the past. Rather, it is an exploration that can enhance your inner world, revealing patterns and insights that shape your present. Through this introspection, you gain a deeper understanding of why you react in particular ways, why certain situations elicit intense emotions, and how these patterns influence your relationships.

Daily journaling prompts are a useful resource for this exploration. They encourage a pause for contemplation, articulating thoughts that often swirl unnoticed in the background of your mind. Begin your morning with a prompt like "What emotions am I experiencing right now, and why?" or conclude your day with "How did I respond to today's challenges?" These inquiries invite honesty and vulnerability. Mind mapping can further enrich this process by visually organizing your thoughts. Initiate with a central theme, such as "self-worth," and expand with related beliefs and experiences. This technique unveils the underlying assumptions guiding your behavior, offering clarity where confusion once prevailed.

Engaging with these exercises may reveal recurring patterns. You might notice a propensity for withdrawal when criticized or an urge to seek reassurance during conflicts. Recognizing these patterns is important for change. It enables you to identify triggers—the situations or moments causing intense emotional reactions—and trace them to their roots. You might discover that a partner's harsh words evoke memories of parental disapproval or that being ignored rekindles feelings of childhood neglect. Grasping these connections offers an opportunity to escape reactive cycles and select healthier responses.

Reflective practices also illuminate self-sabotaging behaviors. These actions often manifest subtly—such as procrastination or avoiding tough conversations—but deeply impact one's ability to cultivate secure attachments. By identifying these behaviors through introspection, one empowers oneself to make conscious decisions aligning with one's values and aspirations. This awareness nurtures personal growth, replacing outdated habits with more constructive ones.

Healing from emotional and psychological trauma is a deeply personal process that unfolds with time, patience, and support. Whether the trauma occurred in childhood or adulthood, its impact does not define your worth or limit your potential for growth. By understanding the roots of trauma and recognizing its signs, you begin to loosen its grip. Through physical movement, meaningful connection, emotional regulation, reflective practices, and professional support, you can rebuild your inner foundation. Therapies like NET, EMDR, and somatic work remind us that healing is not about erasing the past, but about integrating it into a fuller, more empowered sense of self. This chapter has offered tools not just to survive trauma, but to transform it—to find meaning in your experiences and strength in your story. The path may be challenging, but it leads to something powerful: a renewed sense of safety, identity, and hope.

7

Creating A Secure Attachment Style

A secure attachment style is the foundation of healthy relationships and emotional well-being. It is characterized by a balanced, trusting, and empathetic approach to interacting with others. Whether in childhood or adulthood, those with secure attachment feel safe, understood, and valued, which enables them to build lasting connections marked by mutual respect and open communication. In this chapter, this book explores the key indicators of secure attachment, such as comfort with intimacy and independence, effective communication, and emotional regulation, and examines how these traits contribute to both personal growth and relational stability.

A Secure Attachment Style

John Bowlby and Mary Ainsworth, through their studies on children's attachment patterns, identified both secure and insecure attachment types as key elements of their attachment theory. A secure attachment style is defined by a balanced, trusting, and healthy approach to relationships. People—both children and adults —who exhibit a secure attachment style generally feel safe, understood, and appreciated in their relationships. This foundational trust enables them to build lasting connections characterized by mutual respect and empathy (Lein 2024).

Understanding the hallmarks of a secure attachment style can shed light on how healthy relationships function. Below are five key indicators of secure attachment, each illustrated with a real-life example. These traits help identify secure attachment in yourself and others while also serving as a guide for nurturing stronger, more resilient relationships (Lein 2024).

Comfort with Intimacy and Independence

Securely attached individuals are at ease with both closeness and independence. They do not feel threatened when a partner needs space, nor do they become overly preoccupied with the relationship. They are capable of both relying on others and being reliable in return (Lein 2024).

Take Sarah, for example, who exhibits secure attachment, trusts her partner Carlos enough to share her feelings and thoughts while also honoring his need for personal time. This balance allows them to maintain a healthy relationship where both intimacy and independence are respected (Lein 2024).

Healthy Boundaries and Communication

People with secure attachment excel at setting and respecting boundaries. They communicate openly and handle conflicts with calm and constructive dialogue. When someone else establishes a boundary, they respond without overreacting or withdrawing (Lein 2024).

In a recent disagreement, Sarah expressed her concerns clearly and listened attentively to Carlos's perspective. Even when difficult topics were raised, Carlos remained engaged, reinforcing their mutual trust and commitment to resolving issues together (Lein 2024).

Confidence and Self-Worth

Those with a secure attachment typically maintain a positive view of themselves and others. Their confidence in their abilities and inherent worth creates healthy and supportive relationships, attracting others with their positive energy (Lein 2024).

Sarah and Carlos confidently pursue their personal goals and celebrate each other's achievements. They view each other's successes as complementary rather than competitive, which strengthens the supportive dynamic in their relationship (Lein 2024).

Emotional Regulation

A secure attachment style is linked to the ability to manage and regulate emotions effectively. Individuals with this style experience a range of emotions and know how to self-soothe during distress, choosing adaptive coping strategies to handle stress (Lein 2024).

When facing work-related stress, Sarah opts for healthy coping mechanisms like talking with a friend and exercising instead of resorting to destructive behavior. Likewise, Carlos demonstrates adaptive emotional responses during stressful times, contributing to a balanced partnership (Lein 2024).

Reliability and Trust

Securely attached individuals are known for their dependability and honesty. They follow through on commitments and can be trusted to be there when needed, which further strengthens their relationships (Lein 2024).

Sarah is known among her friends and family as someone who consistently shows up when promised. Her reliability and transparent communication about her limits create deep trust and respect within her relationships (Lein 2024).

Research Findings on Securely Attached Individuals

Numerous studies have examined attachment styles across both children and adults, revealing that secure attachment offers significant advantages across various domains—from parenting to professional interactions. Meta-analyses consistently show that securely attached children exhibit enhanced social skills, better quality peer relationships, improved emotional understanding, and stronger language abilities (Lein 2024).

Additionally, secure attachment in childhood is associated with fewer internalizing behaviors and a reduction in externalizing problems. These findings underscore the importance of nurturing secure attachments from an early age, as they lay the groundwork for healthier attachment patterns in adulthood and create a positive feedback loop that benefits individuals throughout their lives (Lein 2024).

In adulthood, individuals with secure attachment tend to recover from stress more effectively and adopt healthy coping strategies to maintain emotional balance. They generally report higher levels of well-being and a more optimistic outlook on life. Their heightened empathy and attunement to others' needs contribute to stronger, more supportive relationships and overall improved mental health. Meanwhile, in romantic relationships, secure attachment is linked with increased satisfaction, stability, and intimacy. Couples who exhibit secure attachment often report greater trust, fewer conflicts, and more effective resolution of disagreements (Lein 2024).

The influence of secure attachment extends into the workplace as well. Research indicates that securely attached individuals tend to perform better on the job, experience lower levels of burnout, and enjoy more positive workplace relationships and overall job satisfaction (Lein 2024).. Moreover, secure attachment is associated with effective leadership and enhanced teamwork; securely attached leaders tend to establish a supportive, empathetic environment that strengthens team cohesion and improves performance (Lein 2024). Overall, these findings highlight the far-reaching impact of secure attachment on an individual's emotional health, quality of interpersonal relationships, and professional success.

Challenges to Secure Attachment

Various experiences throughout childhood, adolescence, or adulthood can disrupt the development of a secure attachment style. Below are some common obstacles that hinder the formation and maintenance of secure attachments:

- **Unresolved Childhood Trauma:** Experiencing emotional neglect, abuse, or inconsistent caregiving in childhood can interfere with the development of secure attachment. Such early trauma often results in difficulties trusting others and regulating emotions, making it harder for individuals to establish stable, secure relationships later in life.
- **Negative Relationship Patterns:** Repeated encounters with manipulation, betrayal, or emotional unavailability in relationships can instill feelings of insecurity and mistrust. Continuous exposure to toxic or unhealthy relationship dynamics tends to reinforce behaviors associated with insecure attachment.
- **Fear of Vulnerability:** A reluctance to open up and be vulnerable with others can obstruct the development of secure attachment. When adults act out of a fear of abandonment, hurt, or rejection, they might avoid intimacy or withdraw emotionally, creating a self-perpetuating cycle of mistrust that is difficult to break.
- **Lack of Positive Role Models:** Without exposure to role models who demonstrate healthy relationships, individuals may struggle to learn how to form secure attachments. The absence of positive examples can make it challenging to develop the skills necessary for building trust, maintaining open communication, and managing emotions effectively.

- **Mental Health Issues:** Struggles with anxiety, depression, or personality disorders can significantly impede the ability to form and sustain secure attachments. Such conditions often impact self-esteem, emotional regulation, and the dynamics of interpersonal relationships, further complicating the establishment of stable bonds.
- **High-Stress Environments:** Constant exposure to high levels of stress—such as financial instability or unsafe living conditions—can undermine secure attachment. Chronic stress diminishes resilience and can lead to increased conflicts in relationships, straining even the strongest bonds (Lein 2024).

Overcoming these challenges is a bit like untangling a knot in your favorite necklace—frustrating at times, and easy to want to give up on, but with patience, care, and sometimes a little help, the delicate links begin to loosen. It often takes conscious effort, growing self-awareness, and sometimes guidance to work through past traumas, reshape relationship patterns, and find steadier ground with our emotions.

Achieving Secure Attachment

Here are several ways you can achieve and establish a secure attachment style:

- **Enhance Self-Awareness and Self-Reflection:** Developing a secure attachment begins with a deep understanding of your own emotions, thoughts, and behaviors in relationships. Start by observing your internal reactions without self-judgment. Ask yourself: Do you tend to withdraw when closeness increases? Do you become anxious when your partner seeks space? Keeping a journal can help you record your responses to various situations, revealing recurring patterns and triggers. You might also try an attachment style assessment to gain initial insights into your current style. Remember, self-reflection is about compassionately understanding your habits so you can choose healthier responses instead of simply reacting.

- **Cultivate Emotional Intelligence:** Building emotional intelligence involves recognizing, understanding, and managing both your own emotions and those of others—a critical skill for secure attachment. Begin by broadening your emotional vocabulary so you can clearly distinguish feelings such as anxiety, frustration, or disappointment. Practicing mindfulness, whether through meditation or regular self-check-ins, helps you become aware of your emotional states and the physical sensations that accompany them. Learn to regulate your emotions—not by suppressing them, but by experiencing them without becoming overwhelmed. Techniques like deep breathing, muscle relaxation, or grounding exercises can be effective. Finally, work on empathy by striving to understand others' perspectives, even when they differ from your own.

- **Establish Trust and Embrace Vulnerability:** Developing secure attachment means taking emotional risks in a safe, gradual manner. Allow yourself to be vulnerable and to trust others, even if past experiences have made this challenging. Begin with small acts of sharing personal thoughts or feelings with someone you trust, such as a friend or family member. In romantic relationships, be open about your needs, express appreciation, and share your dreams and fears. Trust that when someone makes a promise, they mean it, so try to accept their commitment instead of doubting it. Building trust and embracing vulnerability is a skill that grows over time, so be patient with yourself throughout this process.

- **Improve Communication Skills:** Effective communication is essential for secure attachment. This involves not only expressing your needs clearly using "I" statements but also actively listening to others. For example, rather than saying "You never listen to me," try "I feel unheard and need more engagement during our conversations." Practice active listening by focusing entirely on the speaker and reflecting back what you hear to ensure understanding. Learn to handle conflicts constructively by avoiding criticism, defensiveness, contempt, or stonewalling. Remember to be mindful of non-verbal signals like body language and tone of voice, which play a central role in conveying empathy and understanding.

- **Establish and Honor Boundaries:** Maintaining healthy boundaries is key to secure attachment, as it preserves your individuality and respects others' autonomy. Identify what behaviors you find acceptable and those that you don't, and determine what you need to feel safe and respected. Communicate these limits clearly and respectfully, keeping in mind that setting boundaries is about taking care of your own well-being rather than controlling others. Equally, honor the boundaries set by others; if someone asks for space or declines an invitation, respect their needs. Consistency in enforcing your boundaries is essential—if they are repeatedly violated, it might be necessary to reassess the relationship.

- **Practice Consistency and Reliability:** Trust in relationships is built through consistent, reliable actions. Follow through on your commitments—if you say you'll call, do so; if you make plans, keep them. Being punctual and dependable, both in small gestures and significant promises, forms a solid foundation for trust. Emotional consistency is also important: while mood fluctuations are natural, strive to be generally stable and clear about your feelings, especially on challenging days. Show up for others consistently, offer support, and be willing to acknowledge and learn from your mistakes. Consistency isn't about being perfect—it's about establishing a reliable pattern of behavior that reassures those around you (Trammell 2024).

By focusing on these areas—self-awareness, emotional intelligence, vulnerability, communication, boundaries, consistency, and professional support—you can gradually shift toward a more secure attachment style. Though this journey requires time and patience, the resulting benefits in your relationships and overall well-being are well worth the effort.

Co-Creating Secure Attachment in Therapy

Secure attachment is something felt, lived, and co-created within the safety of a new relational experience. While early childhood experiences shape internal models of attachment, these patterns can be reshaped in adulthood, most effectively within the therapeutic relationship. One of the most promising and increasingly recognized approaches to establishing secure attachment in adults is through the therapist intentionally assuming the role of a "good attachment figure," providing a corrective emotional experience that is both relational and reparative (Elliott 2021).

Attachment theory teaches us that people internalize expectations of relationships based on their earliest caregivers. These internal working models are often formed not through explicit narrative memory but instead through affective and sensorimotor experiences that become deeply embedded in the psyche. As a result, insecure attachment in adults reflects adaptations to relational threats or inconsistencies—strategies that once helped the child survive relational distress but may now interfere with the ability to form trusting, reciprocal connections (Elliott 2021).

Psychotherapy offers a unique space in which these internal models can be brought into awareness and, more importantly, transformed. The foundational task of the therapist is to offer a secure base—a trusted presence from which the client can begin to explore painful memories, relational fears, and maladaptive beliefs about self and others. The therapist's role, then, is not only analytical but deeply relational: to embody the very qualities that were missing or inconsistent in the client's early relationships (Elliott 2021).

The Therapist as a Secure Base

The model, often referred to as "therapist-as-good-attachment-figure," centers on this principle. In this approach, the therapist seeks to offer a consistent experience of attunement, responsiveness, emotional availability, and containment. When clients experience the therapist in this way over time, they begin to internalize a different kind of relational reality—one that supports safety, connection, and trust. This new relational experience gradually updates the client's existing internal models, replacing outdated narratives of fear, abandonment, or unworthiness with new templates of secure relating (Elliott 2021).

These positive experiences are emotionally healing, but they also serve a structural function. They help build new representations in the client's mind—ones that reflect safety, responsiveness, and love. In practice, this means the therapist mirrors what an ideal caregiver might provide: careful attention, emotional attunement, protective presence, and reliable care. These interactions provide the foundation for co-creating secure attachment within therapy (Elliott 2021).

Imagery and the Inner World

One particularly powerful method that has emerged for reinforcing this relational healing involves guided imagery. In this practice, the client and therapist collaboratively construct visualized scenarios that evoke experiences of positive attachment. This process operates on multiple levels. Interpersonally, the client engages with internal representations—imagining how it feels to be held, comforted, or seen by a safe attachment figure. Interpersonally, the therapist supports and guides this process with attuned responses. Meta-interpersonally, the client experiences this inner work in the presence of an external, supportive other, allowing for the integration of both internal and external sources of attachment security (Elliott 2021).

This technique draws from the understanding that many attachment experiences, especially early ones, are stored not in verbal or narrative memory but in sensorimotor, affective, and imagistic form. As such, using imagery to access and reshape these representations can be far more effective than insight alone. For example, a client may imagine being held or protected by an ideal caregiver figure, feeling warmth, safety, and soothing. Over time, these emotionally rich and sensory-laden experiences begin to form new memory traces that can compete with or even override the client's earlier, insecure patterns (Elliott 2021).

Importantly, the therapist doesn't simply instruct the client to imagine safety—the safety is co-created. The therapist might ask, "What does it feel like in your body when you imagine this figure looking at you with warmth?" or "Can you let yourself feel how it would be to be completely safe and understood in this moment?" These prompts guide the imagery and reinforce the secure base function of the therapist and help the client stay anchored in a relationally attuned experience (Elliott 2021).

Reappraisal and Restructuring

This process unfolds along two parallel tracks: reappraisal and restructuring. Reappraisal involves cognitively examining the client's current attachment strategies—recognizing how early experiences have shaped relational patterns, beliefs, and defensive adaptations. The therapist supports the client in reflecting on these patterns, helping them see where they might be outdated or misaligned with their current context. For example, a client might come to recognize that their avoidance of closeness is a relic of growing up with emotionally intrusive caregivers, not a necessary protection in their adult relationships (Elliott 2021).

Restructuring, by contrast, is the deeper work of changing the felt sense of what relationships are and what one can expect from others. This change doesn't occur through thought alone. It requires new experiences—emotional, relational, and often nonverbal—that contradict the old models. This is where the therapist's consistent attunement becomes critical. When a client repeatedly experiences the therapist as safe, available, and caring, this begins to create new affective and relational memories that can rewrite older scripts of abandonment, unpredictability, or rejection (Elliott 2021).

Mentalization and Mindfulness

Another key ingredient in this process is mentalization—the capacity to reflect on one's own mental states and those of others. Insecure attachment often coexists with deficits in mentalization, particularly in situations of emotional stress. Helping clients develop this capacity enhances their ability to make sense of their experiences, regulate their emotions, and shift out of automatic, reactive modes of relating (Elliott 2021).

Therapy that emphasizes mentalization doesn't just teach clients to observe their thoughts and feelings. It helps them link these experiences to internal representations and external relational patterns. For instance, a client might learn to notice, "I feel anxious when I don't get a reply right away, and I think it means they're upset with me," and then reflect on how that belief might stem from past experiences of unpredictability or neglect (Elliott 2021).

The more clients are able to observe and reflect on these patterns, the more freedom they gain to respond differently—to pause, ask for clarification, and seek reassurance instead of withdrawing or attacking. In this way, mentalization supports both reappraisal and restructuring, building the reflective capacities that are essential for secure attachment (Elliott 2021).

In therapy, when the client feels warmth, care, and responsiveness from the therapist—not just imagining it but experiencing it viscerally—they begin to form new internal working models. These models are rooted in feeling, in safety, in the body. Over time, this changes the way the client perceives others and relates to them in the real world. They may begin to expect availability rather than rejection, understanding rather than criticism, connection rather than abandonment (Elliott 2021).

This is the heart of co-creating secure attachment: It's not something the therapist gives and not something the client generates alone. It arises in the space between through repeated, emotionally resonant experiences of connection, safety, and care. As these new experiences accumulate, they don't just provide relief; they rebuild the architecture of the client's attachment system (Elliott 2021).

Creating a secure attachment style enriches every aspect of your life. By embracing vulnerability, establishing clear boundaries, and practicing consistent, empathetic communication, you lay the foundation for relationships that are resilient and deeply fulfilling. While challenges like unresolved trauma or negative past relationship patterns can pose obstacles, deliberate self-awareness and professional support can help overcome these hurdles. Ultimately, the skills and insights gained from developing a secure attachment strengthen your relationships and enhance your overall sense of self-worth and well-being. Remember that each step toward secure attachment is an investment in a more connected and empowered future. The following chapter explores ways to reduce overthinking and anxiety and how this can further enhance secure attachment.

8

Reducing Anxiety and Overthinking

R elationship anxiety is more than just occasional insecurity; it is also a persistent state of worry, overthinking, and doubt that can erode the very foundation of your relationships. This chapter discusses the cycle of overanalysis, where you might replay conversations, search for hidden meanings, and question every aspect of your partner's loyalty and your own worth. It explores how these obsessive thoughts, fueled by underlying issues such as anxious attachment, low self-esteem, or even relationship OCD, can escalate into significant distress. Alongside examining the causes and common signs of relationship anxiety, this chapter also focuses on the essential role of trust building in mitigating these fears, empowering you to create a more secure and balanced partnership.

Relationship Anxiety

Relationship anxiety is a state of ongoing worry, excessive overthinking, and nervousness about your romantic connection. It often involves persistent doubts about your partner's loyalty or concerns about whether you are as committed as you should be. While it is normal to have occasional insecurities, for some people, these fears become overwhelming and disruptive (McGrath 2024).

Recognizing when your concerns have escalated is important, especially if you find yourself repeatedly fixated on the same issues to the point of significant distress. In some cases, this can indicate a deeper problem, such as relationship obsessive-compulsive disorder (ROCD), where the intrusive thoughts about your relationship dominate your mind (McGrath 2024).

When relationship anxiety stems from an underlying mental health issue, its impact on your life can be significant. It might interfere with basic functions like eating, sleeping, or focusing, and it can ultimately affect the overall quality of your relationship. The good news is that once you understand what is really happening, effective, evidence-based therapies and support systems can help reduce your anxiety and improve your well-being (McGrath 2024).

Common Signs of Relationship Anxiety

Here are several common signs that you are experiencing relationship anxiety:

- **Doubting Your Partner's True Feelings:** Even if your partner appears loving and caring, you might still feel they don't truly care, and any hint of distance sends your mind into overdrive.
- **Questioning Your Own Value:** You may frequently second-guess whether you matter to your partner, often replaying past interactions in your head to verify your worth.
- **A Constant Need for Reassurance:** Without regular verbal affirmations from your partner, you might spiral into anxious thoughts and constantly seek validation.
- **Preoccupation with Abandonment:** Fears of being left alone can dominate your thoughts, preventing you from fully enjoying the relationship.

- **People-Pleasing Behavior:** To avoid conflict or rejection, you might suppress your own needs and try to keep everything "perfect," which can be emotionally draining.
- **Obsessing over the Future:** While wondering about the future occasionally is normal, if this worry significantly disrupts your day-to-day life, it may be a sign of anticipatory anxiety.
- **Disproportionate Emotional Responses:** Small issues can trigger intense emotional reactions that seem out of proportion to the situation.
- **Self-Sabotaging Actions:** Fear of getting too attached or happy might lead you to push your partner away, start unnecessary conflicts, or withhold your true self (McGrath 2024).

Causes of Relationship Anxiety

There is not one single cause for relationship anxiety. Several factors might contribute, including:

- **An Anxious Attachment Style:** Your early attachment experiences can make you overly sensitive to any perceived emotional distance, leading to constant fears of abandonment.
- **Low Self-Esteem:** Doubting your self-worth can cause you to question your value in the relationship.
- **General Anxiety:** If you already struggle with anxiety in other areas of life, this can easily spill over into your romantic relationships.
- **Relationship OCD (ROCD):** Some individuals develop heightened expectations of what a "perfect" relationship should look like, leading to obsessive concerns and an inability to accept normal relationship struggles (McGrath 2024).

Understanding these aspects of relationship anxiety can help in identifying when your concerns are simply natural insecurities versus when they become overwhelming and require professional attention.

Overcoming Relationship Anxiety

Although it may feel overwhelming in the moment, relationship anxiety is something you can overcome with time and effort. Overcoming it typically requires more than just hearing reassurances that everything is fine in your relationship. Even if you are loved, the persistent anxiety will remain until you truly feel safe and secure. I remember a time when I said "I love you" to my partner with complete sincerity, and yet he still felt uneasy. It wasn't until I explored why he needed to hear it repeatedly to believe it that I realized the issue stemmed from anxious patterns he hadn't yet confronted. Addressing relationship anxiety early on is necessary before it escalates into a bigger problem. Over time, relationship anxiety can result in significant emotional turmoil, decreased motivation, persistent tiredness or burnout, and various physical issues such as stomach discomfort and other related symptoms (Raypole 2024).

Here are some strategies to help you work toward overcoming your relationship anxiety:

- **Preserve your individuality.** As your bond with your partner deepens, you might notice aspects of your identity naturally shifting to accommodate the relationship. While some changes are normal, it's important not to lose sight of who you are. Your partner was drawn to you for your unique qualities, so suppressing these parts of yourself can lead to a diminished sense of self and may even cause your partner to feel they're no longer connecting with the real you.

- **Embrace mindfulness.** Mindfulness involves staying present and aware of your thoughts and feelings without judgment. This practice can help you break free from negative thought spirals, allowing you to focus on your daily interactions with your partner. Even if you worry about the future of your relationship, you can still cherish and enjoy the present moment.

- **Communicate openly.** Often, relationship anxiety originates from internal insecurities rather than actual issues with your partner. However, if certain behaviors—like excessive phone use during conversations or reluctance to engage in family events—trigger your anxiety, it can help to address them openly. Using "I" statements, such as "I feel that there's some distance between us, and it worries me," can create a more constructive dialogue without sounding accusatory. Sharing your feelings, even when you're aware that your partner loves you, can build a stronger connection and provide reassurance.

- **Resist acting on impulsive feelings.** When anxiety arises, the urge to constantly seek proof of your partner's love can be strong. It's natural to want reassurance, but acting on impulsive behaviors—like sending multiple texts asking where they are—can be counterproductive. Instead, try techniques like deep breathing, taking a walk, or calling a close friend to help calm those impulses and maintain a healthy sense of balance.

- **Seek professional guidance.** If managing relationship anxiety on your own becomes too challenging, consider reaching out to a therapist. A professional experienced in couples therapy can help both you and your partner explore your feelings, understand the root causes of your anxiety, and develop effective strategies for managing it. Even a single session focusing on relationship anxiety can provide valuable insights and support (Raypole 2024).

By taking these steps—maintaining your individuality, practicing mindfulness, communicating effectively, resisting impulsive behaviors, and seeking professional help—you can gradually reduce relationship anxiety. This proactive approach will ease your worries and strengthen the foundation of trust and intimacy in your relationship.

Overthinking in Relationships

Have you ever caught yourself mentally replaying a conversation with your partner, dissecting every word for any hidden implication? Do you constantly worry about scenarios that haven't even happened yet? If so, you might be prone to overthinking in your relationship. I remember one evening when my partner sent me a short message saying, "I'd like to talk with you." I spent the whole night worrying that I'd done something wrong, only to discover the next day that he just wanted to discuss how we can take our relationship a step further.

In this context, overthinking is more than just occasional concerns about your relationship. Rather, it involves recurring negative thoughts and anxieties that can deeply affect the health of the partnership. Although it is normal for everyone to overthink from time to time, persistent overanalysis can hinder clear communication, erode trust, and amplify stress—sometimes even over trivial matters (Counseling Center Group 2024).

Overthinking often originates from underlying insecurities and past experiences. For instance, previous relationships marked by betrayal or broken trust can trigger a pattern of overanalyzing, leading you to constantly seek reassurance, scrutinize your partner's behavior for potential signs of disloyalty, or even anticipate the worst outcomes (Counseling Center Group 2024).

The Manifestation of Overthinking

Overthinking in relationships can appear in many forms, shaping how individuals view and engage with their partners. Often, people aren't even aware of how frequently they are caught in a cycle of overanalysis (Counseling Center Group 2024).

For example, you might continuously dissect your partner's words and behaviors, looking for hidden meanings or negative signals. This excessive scrutiny can lead to misunderstandings and conflicts, ultimately undermining effective communication and closeness (Counseling Center Group 2024).

Another manifestation is dwelling on past disputes or unresolved issues. Rehashing old wounds stalls the healing process and stokes lingering resentment, allowing former hurts to dominate current interactions (Counseling Center Group 2024).

Some individuals may also find themselves in a perpetual need for reassurance about their partner's love and commitment, seeking frequent validation due to deep-seated insecurities. If you feel compelled to hear "I love you" repeatedly, it may be a sign of over-thinking (Counseling Center Group 2024).

Being preoccupied with doubts and negative thoughts can prevent you from fully enjoying the present moment. Addressing these tendencies is essential for cultivating a genuine connection and experiencing the true joy and fulfillment that come with a healthy relationship. You deserve to be happy and at peace in your relationship.

Techniques to Break the Cycle of Overthinking

Taking responsibility for your thoughts and actively managing them is essential for curbing overthinking. Although it may seem daunting at first—especially when dealing with long-standing thought patterns—consistent practice can lead to significant improvements. Many recognize that anxiety makes it challenging to take control, yet with the right strategies, you can learn to manage it effectively (Counseling Center Group 2024).

Here are some strategies for overcoming overthinking:

- **Recognize and question your thoughts.** Rather than accepting every thought, especially those that trigger anxiety or negativity, take a step back and examine them. Research in the World Journal of Clinical Cases underscores the importance of cognitive reframing in diminishing negative thinking (Counseling Center Group 2024). Ask yourself, "What evidence supports or refutes this thought?" Often, you'll discover that your worries lack solid justification.
- **Engage in self-reflection.** Understanding the reasons behind your tendency to overthink is necessary. Practices such as journaling, meditation, and therapy can help reveal underlying past hurts and insecurities that fuel your anxiety. These reflective activities enable you to identify and tackle the root causes of unhelpful thought patterns.
- **Focus on the present moment.** Ruminating about the past or worrying about the future only intensifies anxiety. Mindfulness techniques like meditation and deep breathing can help anchor you in the present. By consciously appreciating the positive aspects of your relationship, you can alleviate concerns about potential problems. When your mind starts to spiral, pause, take a few deep breaths, and bring your attention back to the here and now.
- **Establish boundaries for your worries.** Allocating a specific time frame for addressing your worries can be surprisingly effective. For instance, designate a fifteen-minute period each day to focus solely on your concerns. If anxious thoughts arise outside of this window, gently remind yourself to revisit them later. This structured approach helps you maintain control and gradually reduces the frequency of intrusive thoughts (Counseling Center Group 2024).

Interactive Element: Thought-Stopping Practice

Identify a recurring thought that often leads to overthinking. Write it down on a piece of paper. When you notice this thought arising, say "stop" firmly to yourself and visualize crumpling the paper in your mind. Replace the thought with a neutral or positive one, like focusing on your breath or recalling a happy memory. Revisit this exercise frequently to train your brain to establish new, healthier thought patterns, thus reducing the frequency of intrusive, anxiety-inducing thoughts.

Breaking the cycle of overthinking requires practice and patience. By recognizing overthinking patterns and implementing these strategies, you create mental space for clarity and peace. Instead of being trapped in endless loops of thought, you engage with life more fully and authentically. As new habits form, you learn to trust your judgment and your capacity to adapt to whatever life presents.

Trust Building

Trust is the foundation of any secure relationship, acting as a buffer against the doubts and insecurities that invade our minds. When trust is present, it creates a safety net, allowing partners to feel secure and supported. Without it, relationships can become fraught with anxiety and suspicion, eroding the very foundation they stand on. Trust also allows partners to confidently overcome challenges, knowing they can rely on each other. Transparency plays a critical role in enhancing trust, as being open about feelings and intentions creates an environment where honesty thrives. This openness lays the groundwork for mutual respect and understanding.

Mutual understanding is essential for managing overthinking in a relationship. By discussing your anxieties openly and with empathy, you can strengthen your connection and create a secure, supportive partnership. Although these conversations can be challenging, they help prevent misunderstandings by focusing on mutual growth rather than assigning blame. It can be especially tough when your partner struggles to understand your tendency to overthink, but honest dialogue is significant (Counseling Center Group 2024).

Here are the main trust-building strategies:

- **Open and Honest Communication:** Express your feelings and concerns clearly, without casting blame. Use "I" statements to share how you feel—for example, say, "I felt hurt when our anniversary was forgotten," instead of "You always ignore important dates." This approach minimizes defensiveness and encourages productive conversations. If your partner doesn't fully grasp your emotions, it's important to engage in a candid discussion to clarify your perspective.
- **Active Listening and Validation:** Research suggests that feeling heard and respected can even improve sleep quality. Practice active listening by focusing intently on your partner's words, aiming to understand their viewpoint rather than immediately crafting a response. Validating their feelings—even if you don't completely agree—demonstrates respect and helps strengthen your bond. Try not to overthink their responses; simply acknowledge them and keep the conversation open.
- **Establish Relationship Check-ins:** Regular check-ins are valuable for addressing concerns, sharing feelings, and reinforcing your bond. By setting aside dedicated time for these discussions, you build trust and reassurance, which can diminish the need to overanalyze every interaction. If you ever feel that your partner seems distant or indifferent, scheduling a check-in can provide the opportunity to talk it through and restore a sense of security (Counseling Center Group 2024).

While relationship anxiety and overthinking can cast a long shadow over your connection, they are challenges you can overcome. The solution lies in taking a proactive approach—establishing self-aware-ness, practicing mindfulness, and engaging in open, honest communication. By questioning negative thoughts and setting clear boundaries, you gradually reduce anxiety and prevent overthinking from spiraling out of control. Equally important is the ongoing effort to build and reinforce trust, ensuring your relationships feel secure and understood. With the support of professional guidance and consistent, empathetic interactions, you can transform your relationship into a resilient, fulfilling partnership where both trust and genuine connection flourish. In the next chapter, this book highlights the importance of emotional intelligence and its correlation with resilience building to achieve fulfilling attachment.

9

Emotional Intelligence and Building Resilience

E motional intelligence is central for personal well-being, effective leadership, and meaningful interpersonal relationships. It refers to the capacity to recognize, understand, and manage emotions—both our own and those of others. Individuals with high emotional intelligence tend to understand social environments with empathy, self-awareness, and composure, making them more adaptable, resilient, and collaborative. In this chapter, this book explores the core components of emotional intelligence—self-awareness, self-management, social awareness, and relationship management—and how these skills enhance mental health, strengthen communication, and build the foundation for lasting personal and professional success. This chapter also discusses the relationship between emotional intelligence and resilience, exploring how to build resilience and establish a growth mindset.

Emotional Intelligence

Emotional intelligence refers to the ability to recognize and interpret emotions—both in oneself and in others—and to use that awareness to guide thinking and behavior. It encompasses several key domains: perceiving emotions accurately, using emotions to facilitate thought, understanding emotional nuances, and regulating emotional responses effectively (Rao et al. 2024).

This skill set plays a central role across all areas of life. Higher levels of emotional intelligence are associated with better mental health, enhanced personal and professional relationships, and improved functioning in social and occupational settings. Psychological well-being tends to be stronger in individuals who score highly in emotional intelligence (Rao et al. 2024).

The Four Components of Emotional Intelligence

Emotional intelligence is generally divided into four essential areas, and understanding each of these areas is important for developing emotional intelligence (Landry 2024).

Self-Awareness

Self-awareness is the foundation of emotional intelligence. It involves recognizing your own emotions, knowing your strengths and limitations, and understanding how your feelings impact both your behavior and your team's outcomes (Landry 2024).

Research by organizational psychologist Tasha Eurich found that while most people—about 95 percent—believe they're self-aware, only ten to fifteen percent actually are. This disconnect can negatively affect teamwork, often reducing team effectiveness and contributing to stress and low morale (Landry 2024).

To effectively lead others, you must first understand yourself. A helpful way to evaluate your self-awareness is through 360-degree feedback, where you assess your performance and compare it with feedback from managers, colleagues, and subordinates. This process can uncover how you're viewed by others and highlight areas for growth (Landry 2024).

Self-Management

Self-management is your ability to control your emotions—especially under pressure—and maintain a positive attitude when things don't go as planned (Landry 2024). I remember a moment in my early career when I was faced with a difficult presentation. As the pressure mounted, I felt myself becoming overwhelmed and ready to react impulsively. Instead of reacting immediately, I paused and took a few deep breaths, allowing myself a moment of reflection. This moment of self-management helped me approach the situation with a clear mind, and I was able to make decisions that resolved the issue and kept my relationships with my colleagues intact. It was a turning point where I realized the power of emotional regulation in high-pressure situations

Unlike instinctive reactions, emotionally intelligent responses are thoughtful and deliberate. Developing this skill involves taking a moment to pause, breathe, and regroup—whether that means taking a break or speaking with someone you trust—so you can respond calmly and effectively to difficult situations (Landry 2024).

Social Awareness

Understanding others is just as important as understanding yourself. Social awareness is about being attuned to the emotions of those around you and understanding the social dynamics within your environment (Landry 2024).

Empathy is at the heart of social awareness. Effective leaders listen and consider the emotions and viewpoints of others, which helps them collaborate and communicate more successfully (Landry 2024).

According to leadership firm DDI, empathy is the most important leadership skill. Leaders who demonstrate empathy perform over 40 percent better in areas like coaching, engagement, and decision-making. Similarly, the Center for Creative Leadership found that managers who show empathy are rated more highly by their supervisors. By practicing empathy, you strengthen your team and enhance your own leadership abilities (Landry 2024).

Relationship Management

This component focuses on how well you build and maintain positive interactions—whether it's coaching team members, resolving conflicts, or providing support. Avoiding conflict may seem easier, but unresolved issues often lead to wasted time—about eight hours per conflict, according to research—through gossip or other unproductive behaviors, which ultimately harms team morale and efficiency (Landry 2024).

Strong leaders tackle issues directly and respectfully. A survey from the Society for Human Resource Management found that 72 percent of employees consider respectful treatment of everyone, regardless of rank, to be the most important factor in job satisfaction. Addressing problems openly and establishing mutual respect are key to maintaining a healthy and productive work environment (Landry 2024).

Enhancing Emotional Intelligence

Here are some ways you can develop emotional intelligence skills:

- **Keep a Journal:** Make it a habit to write about how your emotions impacted your decisions, interactions, and meetings each day. Reflecting on both the positives and negatives can help you recognize patterns and adjust your behavior moving forward.
- **Try a 360-Degree Review:** Seek input from your supervisor, coworkers, and team members while also completing a self-evaluation. Comparing the feedback can reveal areas where your perception differs from how others see you, helping identify leadership blind spots.

- **Engage in Active Listening:** Minimize distractions and focus completely on the speaker. Show that you're present by summarizing what's been said and using body language like nodding to demonstrate your attentiveness.
- **Tune Into Your Emotions:** When you feel a strong emotional reaction, pause to consider its source and what triggered it. This reflection helps you better understand your own emotions and build empathy for others.
- **Enroll in a Course or Workshop:** Consider taking an online program, such as the Leadership Principles course from HBS Online, which includes tools like 360-degree assessments to help you gain deeper insight into your emotional strengths and areas for growth (Landry 2024).

These basic practices in self-awareness and empathy provide a strong starting point for developing emotional intelligence.

Resilience

Resilience refers to a person's ability and capacity to effectively adapt when faced with adversity, trauma, tragedy, threats, or major stressors. It is not a fixed trait but a dynamic process influenced by biological, psychological, social, and environmental elements that help individuals maintain mental health despite experiencing hardship at any stage of life. In other words, resilience is something that can be developed by anyone, regardless of age or circumstance. While resilience can be created, various biological and psychosocial factors can influence it—either enhancing or hindering its development (Rao et al. 2024).

Factors That Enhance Resilience

Resilience is supported by several positive attributes. These include secure attachment and bonding, high intelligence, and well-developed social skills. Good physical health and an adaptable, easygoing temperament also contribute positively. Individuals who are socially approachable, possess a healthy self-image and self-awareness, and display optimism along with a sense of humor tend to be more resilient. Other contributing factors include being productive, having a clear sense of purpose, being organized, and being capable of compartmentalizing emotions. Engaging in recreation, demonstrating cognitive flexibility, and employing active coping strategies further strengthen a person's resilience (Rao et al. 2024).

Factors That Hinder Resilience

Conversely, certain negative influences can undermine the development of resilience. Poor perinatal care and adverse experiences during childhood can set a challenging foundation. Dysfunctional family dynamics and the presence of psychopathology in parents may further impede emotional and psychological growth. Inadequate schooling and the absence of positive role models or mentors also play a significant role. Additionally, being raised in environments marked by violence or being exposed to traumatic events such as wars and natural disasters can severely impact an individual's capacity to build and sustain resilience (Rao et al. 2024).

Interactive Element: Resilience-Building Challenges

Consider engaging in resilience-building challenges that stretch your comfort zone. These activities include learning a new skill, volunteering in unfamiliar settings, or tackling a physical challenge, like hiking a difficult trail. These experiences build confidence and demonstrate your capacity to overcome adversity.

Reflective journaling is another powerful tool for developing resilience. Take time to write about past recoveries from setbacks. Focus on what helped you bounce back and what you learned. This exercise reinforces the idea that you've navigated challenges and can do so again.

An example of this is recalling a time you overcame a significant challenge, noting the specific emotions and doubts you experienced at the time. Reflect on the strategies you used to navigate this challenge and how these can be applied to current or future struggles. This type of reflection promotes personal growth and provides reassurance of your capability to handle adversity.

Incorporating these practices into your life creates a robust foundation for emotional resilience. They empower you to face life's uncertainties confidently and gracefully, transforming obstacles into stepping stones toward personal growth and fulfillment.

Correlations Between Resilience and Emotional Intelligence

It is no surprise that people who are more in tune with their emotions often bounce back more easily from life's setbacks. Emotional intelligence and resilience go hand in hand—when you understand your emotions and can manage them well, you're better equipped to handle tough times (Rao et al. 2024). I've found that simply being able to name what I'm feeling in a stressful moment helps me respond in a calmer, more grounded way. For instance, a few years ago, I was overwhelmed by work and personal commitments, feeling a mix of frustration and anxiety. Instead of letting those emotions spiral, I took a moment to recognize and name them, which helped me respond more calmly. Also, reaching out to a friend for support reminded me that emotional intelligence isn't just about managing emotions—it's also about connecting with others and choosing healthier coping strategies. This kind of awareness makes it easier to pause, take a breath, and choose how to react instead of spiraling.

Emotional intelligence isn't just about self-awareness, though. It also deepens our empathy, which strengthens our relationships and gives us a solid support system when things get hard. And when we can regulate our emotions, we're more likely to turn to healthy coping tools—like laughter, perspective, or simply reaching out—rather than getting stuck in negativity. Interestingly, resilience can also feed back into emotional intelligence. When we practice kindness, stay hopeful, or find meaning in challenges, we're not just surviving—

we're building emotional muscles that help us thrive. Traits like self-motivation and a sense of purpose aren't just nice to have—they're part of what makes us feel more connected, satisfied, and ready to face whatever comes next (Rao et al. 2024).

How Emotional Intelligence Can Strengthen Resilience

You can strengthen their resilience by applying emotional intelligence in various practical ways. One of the most effective strategies is developing self-awareness (Ei4Change n.d.). When I can recognize what I'm feeling and why—whether it's stress, fear, or frustration—I'm much better at figuring out what I need in that moment. That kind of self-awareness helps me catch unhelpful patterns, set healthy boundaries, and lean on the people I trust when things get rough.

Learning to regulate emotions is also important. It is not always easy to stay calm under pressure, but with practice—through things like journaling, mindful movement, or even just a few deep breaths—I've learned to pause before reacting. It doesn't mean I don't feel overwhelmed sometimes, but I'm less likely to let those emotions take over.

Staying motivated also plays a central part in resilience (Ei4Change n.d.). Setting small, meaningful goals keeps me grounded and gives me something to hold onto, especially when life feels uncertain. And then there's empathy—not just toward others, but toward myself too. When I'm able to really listen, connect, and show compassion, it creates a sense of belonging and support that makes even the hardest days feel a little lighter.

Fundamentally, resilience isn't something you either have or you don't. It's something you build over time—by tuning into your emotions, caring for your mental well-being, and staying open to the messy, beautiful process of growth.

Creating a Growth Mindset

A growth mindset is the belief that your abilities can develop through effort and practice, even if you initially find something difficult. Individuals with this mindset see obstacles and failures as chances to learn and improve, trusting that perseverance will lead to success. In contrast, a fixed mindset is the belief that intelligence and abilities are static and cannot be changed over time (Purdue Global 2024).

Research shows that having a growth mindset offers several advantages:

- A global study by the Organization for Economic Cooperation and Development revealed that students with a growth mindset tend to perform better on tests and report higher well-being.
- According to Harvard Business Review, supervisors in companies that encourage a growth mindset view their employees more positively than those in fixed-mindset organizations. They see them as more creative, cooperative, and eager to develop, and are more likely to believe their employees have leadership potential.
- The journal Brain Sciences notes that individuals with a growth mindset often improve without external rewards, show greater motivation, achieve more academically, and handle academic challenges more effectively (Purdue Global 2024).

If you tend to lean toward a fixed mindset, it's still entirely possible to shift your perspective. To cultivate a growth mindset, consider these steps:

- **Recognize your current mindset.** You can't change what you're unaware of. Start by observing your thoughts and reactions when things go wrong or challenges arise.

- **Reframe challenges as learning opportunities.** Tell yourself you welcome the challenge because it's a chance to grow. It might feel unnatural at first, but repeating this message can reshape your outlook.
- **Be kind to yourself—growth takes time.** Developing a growth mindset won't happen instantly. Expect ups and downs and remember that progress is part of a long-term journey.
- **Concentrate on actions over inherent qualities.** Focusing too much on traits like talent can reinforce a fixed mindset. Instead, take steps toward your goals and acknowledge your efforts along the way.
- **Connect with people who embrace a growth mindset.** Talk to those who have made the shift themselves — they may offer useful advice or encouragement.
- **Shift how you view failure.** As Alexander Fleming, who discovered penicillin, put it, failure can lead to discovery (Purdue Global 2024). Start thinking of failure as a stepping stone to learning something new.
- **Put your goals in writing.** Studies show that writing down your goals increases the likelihood of achieving them. Be clear about what you aim to accomplish.
- **Celebrate others' achievements.** Success isn't a limited resource. Congratulate others on their accomplishments and learn from their experiences.
- **Seek constructive feedback.** People close to you might notice things you miss. Treat their input as helpful insight, not personal criticism.
- **Use the word "yet."** When you're struggling with something, remind yourself you're not good at it *yet*. This simple word signals that growth is possible with time and practice (Purdue Global 2024).

Embracing Progress

Recognizing personal progress is a powerful act of self-affirmation. It is about acknowledging every step, no matter how small, that propels you toward your goals. Celebrating these wins is not just about patting yourself on the back, but it is also about reinforcing your sense of capability and motivating you to continue forging ahead. When you identify and appreciate these small victories, you create a positive feedback loop. This boosts your confidence and fuels your determination to keep striving for more. Small wins are often the building blocks of more significant achievements. They deserve recognition.

Integrating Celebration into Daily Life

The psychological benefits of recognizing progress are substantial. Celebrating achievements, even minor ones, releases dopamine in the brain, which increases feelings of pleasure and satisfaction. This chemical shift encourages a positive mindset, making it easier to tackle future challenges with optimism and resilience. By acknowledging progress, you create an internal narrative highlighting growth over perfection, thus reducing the likelihood of burnout and frustration.

Tracking growth is essential for maintaining momentum on your path to personal development. Progress journals or growth charts can be useful resources in this process. You create a tangible record of how far you have come by chronologically documenting your achievements. This visual representation reminds you of your capability and resilience during moments of doubt or discouragement.

Setting personal goals and regularly reviewing them is another effective method for tracking growth. Establish clear, achievable objectives and periodically assess your progress. Adjust these goals as needed to align with your evolving aspirations. Also, reflect on past successes in terms of the end results and what these victories mean to you and your personal growth. This reflection helps to identify core values and strengths, reinforcing confidence and establishing a deep sense of self-worth.

Reflection plays a central role in celebrating growth, offering an opportunity to appreciate your journey. Reflective journaling allows you to examine your personal achievements in depth. By writing about what you have accomplished and how you reached each milestone, you gain insight into the strategies and attitudes that have served you well. This reflection reinforces positive behaviors and helps identify areas for further improvement. Sharing your progress with supportive friends or mentors can also magnify the impact of your accomplishments. These individuals offer validation and encouragement, strengthening your motivation to pursue your goals.

Celebrating accomplishments can be enriched by rituals and activities that honor your growth journey. Consider creating a personal achievement scrapbook where you compile notes, photos, and mementos related to significant milestones. This creative endeavor commemorates your successes and provides a visual reminder of your achievements. Organizing a celebration or ritual to mark milestones is another way to honor your progress. Whether it is a simple dinner with loved ones or a more elaborate event, such celebrations reinforce the significance of your achievements and provide an opportunity to express gratitude for the support you have received along the way. Design celebrations that resonate personally, whether it involves physical mementos, experiential rewards, or sharing moments with others. This diversity in celebration acknowledges the unique ways people find joy and satisfaction, guaranteeing that literary accomplishments feel meaningful and personalized.

Emotional intelligence is not a fixed trait but a dynamic set of skills that can be cultivated over time with intention and practice. By developing self-awareness, regulating emotional responses, empathizing with others, and building healthy relationships, individuals enhance their personal growth and their resilience in the face of adversity. These competencies are deeply interconnected, reinforcing one another to create a strong emotional foundation.

Whether navigating daily stressors or leading through complex challenges, emotionally intelligent individuals are better equipped to thrive with clarity, compassion, and confidence. As explored in this chapter, investing in emotional intelligence is not just beneficial—it's essential for leading a fulfilling and resilient life.

10

Sustaining Change and Growth

C hange is often easy to initiate but difficult to sustain. While short-term improvements may offer quick results, true transformation lies in the ability to maintain meaningful progress over time. Understanding long-term change means recognizing that sustained growth is a dynamic, ongoing process—one that requires thoughtful planning, emotional resilience, and a commitment to personal development. Whether someone is striving for better health, stronger relationships, or professional advancement, long-term change demands more than momentary willpower. It calls for a shift in mindset, habits, and environment (Sivakumar 2025).

After years of struggling with failed relationships rooted in my own anxious attachment patterns, it took me time to realize I was finally ready for a relationship built on healthy boundaries, mutual independence, and a strong sense of self-worth. Actual, lasting change and growth don't happen overnight, but the journey has been incredibly fulfilling and worthwhile every step of the way.

This chapter explores the key components that support lasting change, including identifying relapse triggers, building a strong support network, and practicing self-compassion. It also emphasizes the importance of adaptability, self-reflection, and a growth-oriented mindset. By unpacking these interconnected elements, readers can develop a deeper understanding of what it takes not just to initiate change, but to sustain it for a lifetime.

Understanding Long-Term Change

Long-term change involves making enduring adjustments in your behavior, mindset, and lifestyle to improve overall well-being. Rather than relying on short-term fixes, this kind of transformation encourages you to adopt lasting strategies that support meaningful personal development. Whether in the context of health, career, or relationships, long-term change will empower you to adapt and thrive in an ever-evolving world (Sivakumar 2025).

Despite its benefits, sustaining change over time presents several challenges. External influences, such as cultural expectations, and internal obstacles, such as deeply rooted habits or self-doubt, can make consistency difficult. Everyone experiences periods of low motivation or wavering commitment, which often results in reverting to old patterns. Acknowledging and understanding these recurring cycles is essential to effectively breaking them (Sivakumar 2025).

Psychological elements also play a central role in maintaining change. Traits such as emotional resilience, self-efficacy, and a growth mindset can greatly influence your ability to stay on course. Resilience will help you recover from setbacks, while self-efficacy will strengthen your confidence in your own ability to achieve goals. A growth mindset, in turn, will promote adaptability and a willingness to embrace learning, making it easier for you to persevere through challenges (Sivakumar 2025).

Successfully navigating long-term change requires deliberate strategies, consistency, and a deep understanding of the internal and external factors that impact progress. Establishing a supportive environment and applying evidence-based techniques to reinforce new habits can make this journey more manageable. I truly believe that developing an awareness of what sustains long-term transformation will pave the way for meaningful and lasting personal growth.

Identifying Triggers That Lead to Relapse

Recognizing the triggers that may lead to relapse is necessary for maintaining long-term change and successfully sustaining transformation. These triggers can be categorized into emotional, environmental, and social cues.

Emotional triggers often arise from feelings such as stress, anxiety, or sadness, causing individuals to revert to old habits for temporary relief. Identifying these emotional signals is an important step if you are looking to maintain your progress and prevent setbacks (Sivakumar 2025). For instance, I used to crave junk food whenever I felt stressed after work. It wasn't until I started journaling that I recognized this emotional trigger. I realized it wasn't hunger – it was anxiety. Replacing that habit with a short walk or breathing exercise helped shift the pattern

Environmental triggers include specific places or situations that remind you of past behaviors. For instance, if you are working to adopt a healthier lifestyle, you might find that certain social environments or locations trigger cravings or temptations. By being aware of these environmental cues, you can either avoid them or develop strategies to cope with them, reinforcing your commitment to change (Sivakumar 2025).

Social triggers also have a significant impact on relapse. Interactions with family, friends, or peers can either support or hinder your new habits. Social settings often bring up memories or emotions tied to old behaviors. Therefore, it is essential to recognize which relationships or social situations may influence your decision-making. Evaluating your own social circle and seeking out support can help you reinforce positive habits and prevent falling back into previous patterns (Sivakumar 2025).

To effectively manage these triggers, you can implement several strategies. Keeping a journal to record emotions and situations that provoke cravings can help raise awareness of these patterns. Additionally, practicing mindfulness can allow you to recognize your reactions to triggers in the moment, giving yourself the power to make healthier choices rather than reverting to old habits. By understanding and managing these triggers, you can create a stronger foundation for long-term change and guarantee that you remain on track with your transformative journey (Sivakumar 2025).

The Importance of Relapse Prevention Planning

Planning for relapse is a vital part of sustaining long-term progress in areas such as personal development, health, and behavior change. Taking a proactive approach will allow you to prepare for potential setbacks and reinforce your ability to stay on course. A major first step in relapse prevention is identifying situations that pose a high risk for regression. Being aware of specific triggers—whether emotional states, environments, or circumstances—allows you to anticipate and manage moments when you feel most vulnerable to slipping back into old patterns (Sivakumar 2025).

Equally important is the implementation of healthy coping strategies. This can help you manage emotional stress, anxiety, and other psychological challenges that might threaten you progress. Techniques such as mindfulness, regular physical exercise, and journaling are effective ways that you can enhance your emotional stability and promote continued growth. By embedding these practices into your everyday life, you strengthen your ability to handle adversity and maintain your progress (Sivakumar 2025).

Building a reliable support system also plays a key role in relapse prevention. Connecting with empathetic and supportive people—be it friends, family, or members of a support group—can boost your motivation and reinforce accountability. These relationships create a buffer against setbacks by offering you encouragement and shared understanding (Sivakumar 2025).

Finally, it's essential to routinely revisit and adjust your relapse prevention plan. As life evolves, new challenges may arise that require updated strategies. Regular reflection ensures the plan remains adaptive, practical, and aligned with your current goals and needs (Sivakumar 2025).

Sustaining Momentum

Sustaining meaningful change over the long term often requires intentional strategies that reinforce dedication. One highly effective method is setting specific and actionable goals. Clear, measurable objectives help focus efforts and allow you to monitor your progress with greater accuracy. For example, rather than making a general goal such as "be healthier," you might set a target like "walk thirty minutes daily," which offers a concrete benchmark to stay motivated and accountable (Sivakumar 2025).

Positive affirmations also play a valuable role in maintaining commitment. These brief, empowering statements support a change-oriented mindset by counteracting self-doubt and reinforcing self-belief. By regularly repeating affirmations like "I am strong and capable of change" you can enhance inner confidence and resilience, particularly during difficult moments (Sivakumar 2025).

Another essential strategy involves creating accountability through partnerships or group involvement. When you share your goals with someone else, you will often feel a heightened sense of responsibility to follow through. This accountability might come from a friend checking in regularly, a mentor providing guidance, or a support group offering shared encouragement. Such connections will keep you focused and deepen your engagement with the change process (Sivakumar 2025).

When these strategies—goal setting, affirmations, and accountability—are woven into your daily routine, they help solidify long-term transformation. For example, a few years ago, I set a goal to walk 30 minutes daily. It was challenging at first, but the sense of accomplishment after each walk helped me regain motivation and momentum, even on tough days. Through consistent practice, you can reinforce your commitment, stay aligned with your intentions, and build momentum toward lasting change.

Building a Support System

Creating a strong support system is key to sustaining positive change. Friends, family, and peers play a vital role in influencing your ability to maintain behavioral and lifestyle shifts. A supportive network offers a sense of belonging and encouragement, especially during difficult moments. Support can come in many forms, from participating in shared healthy activities to providing emotional backing during setbacks (Sivakumar 2025).

Choosing companions who align with your values and goals is critical. Collaborating with others—whether by attending group workouts or preparing nutritious meals together—can make the process enjoyable and more sustainable. Support groups also offer a broader community of individuals who share similar goals to you and can provide unique insights based on their own experiences (Sivakumar 2025).

Openly discussing challenges and progress can reduce feelings of isolation. Realizing others face similar hurdles establishes a sense of connection and shared purpose. Celebrating wins and navigating obstacles together can deepen relationships and promote learning and resilience. Consistent communication—whether through regular meetings, video calls, or online communities—is central for maintaining motivation and a sense of togetherness throughout the journey. Ultimately, a dependable support network lays the groundwork for continuous growth and reinforces commitment to personal transformation (Sivakumar 2025).

Practicing Self-Compassion

Self-compassion is a foundation of long-term change. It involves treating oneself with kindness and patience during times of struggle or failure. By cultivating a compassionate inner voice, individuals can soften harsh self-judgment and reduce feelings like guilt or shame that often accompany setbacks. This supportive mindset helps build resilience and sustained motivation (Sivakumar 2025).

One way to nurture self-compassion is through mindful awareness —recognizing emotions without judgment and understanding that setbacks are part of the human experience. Realizing that everyone encounters challenges helps normalize the process and establishes a sense of solidarity (Sivakumar 2025).

Positive affirmations are another helpful tool. Crafting and repeating uplifting statements about your strengths and value can replace negative internal dialogue with encouragement. Over time, this practice strengthens emotional resilience and supports recovery after setbacks (Sivakumar 2025).

Adopting a growth mindset also reinforces self-compassion. Viewing challenges as opportunities to learn willl encourage you to remain committed despite obstacles. This approach transforms difficulties into stepping stones for improvement and makes the path to transformation more sustainable. By embracing self-compassion, you can create a nurturing internal environment that fuels perseverance and ongoing development (Sivakumar 2025).

Tracking Progress and Recognizing Milestones

Maintaining progress over the long term requires ongoing evaluation and acknowledgment of achievements. Monitoring personal growth helps assess what is working and also boosts morale by highlighting progress (Sivakumar 2025).

Journaling remains a valuable method for documenting your thoughts, feelings, and accomplishments. Reflecting on entries can provide insight into the journey and inspire continued effort. In addition, digital tools and goal-tracking apps can offer structured ways to measure progress, visualize milestones, and receive timely reminders to stay on track (Sivakumar 2025).

Celebrating small successes is equally important. Each achievement, no matter how minor, reinforces forward movement and strengthens commitment. These celebrations can take various forms— rewarding yourself with a treat, sharing news with friends, or simply taking a moment to acknowledge your hard work. Recognizing progress and taking time to celebrate it encourages a more positive and rewarding change process, keeping enthusiasm and commitment alive (Sivakumar 2025).

Flexibility and Adaptability in the Face of Change

Embracing change and staying adaptable is essential for long-term success. Flexibility enables you to respond effectively to the unpredictability that often accompanies personal transformation. This means being open to adjusting your routines and exploring new strategies when needed. Challenges are inevitable, but maintaining a flexible mindset reduces frustration and creates resilience. Seeing setbacks as learning opportunities will allow you to remain engaged and proactive instead of feeling stuck (Sivakumar 2025).

Adaptability also promotes creative problem-solving and invites new ideas and experiences into the transformation process. Being open to change expands possibilities and can make your journey more fulfilling. Practical ways to build your adaptability include regular self-assessment and engaging in conversations with trusted peers who can offer alternative viewpoints. A growth mindset also supports flexibility, as it encourages you to see change as a constant and valuable part of life. By staying flexible and responsive, you can sustain progress and better navigate the evolving nature of personal transformation (Sivakumar 2025).

Establishing a Long-Term Change Mindset

A sustained change mindset is essential if you want to maintain lasting transformation. This mindset is rooted in the pursuit of continuous improvement and a commitment to evolving over time. With this perspective, you are better equipped to face challenges and remain focused on their goals (Sivakumar 2025).

Central to this mindset is the belief in personal growth—the idea that abilities can be developed through effort and perseverance. With this outlook, you are more likely to overcome difficulties, as they see them as chances to learn rather than as permanent setbacks (Sivakumar 2025).

Establishing clear, achievable goals is also key. Defined objectives provide direction and a way to measure progress, helping you stay motivated. Using tools like journals or digital planners can make tracking easier and more effective (Sivakumar 2025).

Equally important is the presence of a support network. Connecting with others who share your vision provides encouragement and a sense of accountability. Sharing your journey with a community can inspire continued progress and mutual motivation (Sivakumar 2025).

In sum, establishing a mindset focused on growth, goal setting, and support sets the stage for long-term success. It promotes personal development and contributes to a deeper sense of purpose and well-being (Sivakumar 2025).

Daily Reflection, Lasting Insight

Reflective journaling is a useful way to enhance self-awareness and gain personal insight. By documenting thoughts and emotions, you create introspection that reveals the patterns shaping your experiences. This solidifies your self-understanding, offering clarity over time. Collating your experiences provides insights that might otherwise go unnoticed, illuminating your path toward sustained growth.

To guide this process, you might consider utilizing prompts to direct reflection. Begin with gratitude exercises, noting three things each day that evoke thankfulness. This practice shifts focus from scarcity to abundance, establishing a fulfillment mindset. Explore core values by asking questions like, "What do I stand for?" or "How do my actions align with my core beliefs?" These questions convey significant exploration, helping you connect with your authentic self and guide your own decisions.

Consistency is necessary in journaling. Establish a routine suited to your lifestyle, perhaps writing each morning or before bed. Overcoming barriers to regular practice involves setting reminders or designating specific time slots. Remember, it is about persistence —even brief entries contribute to self-discovery journeys.

Long-term change is less about reaching a final destination and more about embracing an evolving process of growth and self-discovery. It requires consistent effort, strategic planning, and emotional flexibility. Along the way, individuals will encounter setbacks, resistance, and moments of doubt. However, these challenges are not signs of failure, but rather, they are opportunities to reflect, learn, and adjust course.

By identifying triggers, practicing relapse prevention, setting intentional goals, and creating a supportive environment, individuals can build the resilience and clarity needed to stay aligned with their vision. Integrating self-compassion and reflective practices further nurtures the mindset necessary for sustainable transformation. Ultimately, understanding and implementing the principles of long-term change allows individuals to create a foundation for a more purposeful, balanced, and fulfilling life.

How You Can Help Other People

Change is coming, but it won't happen overnight. You're going to need to keep working at it to reach the level of security and peace of mind you long for. You're well on your way, though, and that makes you the perfect person to help other people who are just at the start of this journey.

Simply by sharing your honest opinion of this book and a little about how it's helped you, you'll show new readers that change is possible—and you'll show them exactly where they can find the guidance they need to get started.

Scan the QR code below to leave your review on Amazon

Thank you so much for your support. Here's to an authentic, fulfilling, and secure future!

Conclusion

This book has explored a deep understanding of anxious attachment and its impact on relationships. It has also underscored how you can move away from anxious attachment by building foundations of secure, healthy relationships.

First, this book has taught you how to recognize the origins of anxious attachment and how it influences your behavior. Second, this book has explored emotional regulation techniques, equipping you with tools to manage your feelings constructively. It has focused on building self-worth and independence, emphasizing the importance of internal validation over external approval. Third, this book established the importance of communication skills, teaching you to express your needs assertively and listen actively. Fourth, this book also discussed boundary-setting to safeguard your emotional well-being and addressed healing past traumas to reshape narratives for a healthier self-view. Finally, this book emphasized how you can sustain the change and growth you have experienced, creating a more fulfilling future.

Some key lessons you have taken away from this book include the power of self-awareness in identifying patterns and triggers, the importance of regulating your emotions with intention, and the strength of self-compassion. You have also seen how trust and vulnerability pave the way for meaningful, authentic relationships. These insights are ready to be applied in everyday life.

Looking ahead, remember that lasting change is built on consistency. The exercises and practices you have explored here are habits to weave into your daily routine. Whether it is through mindful breathing, journaling, boundary-setting, or moments of reflection, these exercises will continue to support your growth. Each small step you take reinforces the transformation you have undertaken. You have what it takes to move beyond anxious attachment and create relationships rooted in love, trust, and authenticity. Let this newfound confidence guide you and remind you of your strength and your capacity to form connections that are both safe and deeply fulfilling.

I encourage you to keep growing. Seek out new resources, surround yourself with supportive people, and stay open to learning. Personal development is a lifelong journey, with every challenge you face and every insight you gain adding depth and meaning to your life. The life and love you are seeking are within reach, already taking shape through every intentional choice you make. With continued practice, self-reflection, and compassion, you can meet life's ups and downs with grace and resilience. You are worthy. You are capable. And you are more than deserving of the joy, peace, and authentic relationships that await. Your growth matters, even when it feels slow or unseen. Progress is not always loud; sometimes it is in the quiet moments of choosing yourself.

Here's to the journey ahead—may it be filled with growth, discovery, and a deep sense of wholeness.

References

American Psychological Association. 2025. "Narrative exposure therapy (NET)." https://www.apa.org/ptsd-guideline/treatments/narrative-exposure-therapy#:~

Better Health Channel. n.d. "Relationships and communication." https://www.betterhealth.vic.gov.au/health/healthyliving/relationships-and-communication#some-things-are-difficult-to-communicate.

Body & Mind. n.d. "Breathing techniques to calm your body and mind." https://bodymindonline.com.au/3-breathing-techniques/.

Cherry, Kendra. 2025. "What happens when you embrace autonomy—and how to be more autonomous: A complete guide to self-control." Very Well Mind. https://www.verywellmind.com/autonomy-in-psychology-how-to-make-your-own-choices-7496882#toc-what-makes-a-person-autonomous.

Cikanavicius, Darius. 2017. "The trap of external validation for self-esteem." PsychCentral. https://psychcentral.com/blog/psychology-self/2017/08/validation-self-esteem#1.

Cognitive Behavioral Therapy Los Angeles. n.d. "Mindfulness STOP skill." https://cogbtherapy.com/mindfulness-meditation-blog/mindfulness-stop-skill.

Copley, Laura. 2024. "Anxious attachment style: What it is (+ its hidden strengths)." Positive Psychology. https://positivepsychology.com/anxious-attachment-style/.

Counseling Center Group. 2024. "Understanding and supporting overthinkers in relationships." https://counselingcentergroup.com/overthinkers-in-relationships/.

Dole, Kate. 2018. "88 affirmations for skeptics and cynics—LikelyTale.com." Medium. https://medium.com/likely-tale/88-affirmations-for-skeptics-and-cynics-likelytale-com-b26ec86dbed9.

Ei4Change. n.d. "The link between emotional intelligence and resilience." https://ei4change.com/the-link-between-emotional-intelligence-and-resilience/#:~

Elliott, David S. 2021. "Co-creating secure attachment imagery to enhance relational healing." New Directions in Psychotherapy and Relationship Psychoanalysis 15: 36-55. https://www.davidelliottphd.com/wp-content/uploads/2022/05/Elliott.AttachmentRelationalHealing.pdf.

Foundation Asheville. n.d. "Internal vs. external validation for self esteem growth." https://foundationsasheville.com/internal-vs-external-validation-for-self-esteem-growth/.

Girolimon, Mars. January 19, 2024. "50 Best Personal Growth Quotes for Everyday Evolution." Southern New Hampshire University. Accessed March 31, 2025. https://www.snhu.edu/about-us/newsroom/education/personal-growth-quotes.

Headspace. 2023. "What is mindfulness?" https://www.headspace.com/mindfulness/mindfulness-101.

Hill, Tamara. 2018. "Toxic behaviors: 12 examples of unhealthy boundaries."

PsychCentral. https://psychcentral.com/blog/caregivers/2018/08/toxic-behav iors-12-examples-of-unhealthy-boundaries#1.

Klynn, Bethany. 2024. "Emotional regulation: Skills, exercises, and strategies." BetterUp. https://www.betterup.com/blog/emotional-regulation-skills.

Lamothe, Cindy. 2025. "How to improve communication in a relationship." Healthline. https://www.healthline.com/health/lack-of-communication.

Landry, Lauren. 2024. "Why emotional intelligence is important in leadership." Harvard Business School. https://online.hbs.edu/blog/post/emotional-intelli gence-in-leadership.

Lein, Andrea. 2024. "Secure attachment style: Why it matters & how to nurture it." Positive Psychology. https://positivepsychology.com/secure-attachment-style/.

Lyons, Anita. 2018. "Why Hannah Gadsby's message about self-deprecating humour made me listen." Yahoo. https://au.lifestyle.yahoo.com/hannah-gadsbys-message-self-deprecating-humour-made-listen-035448388.html.

Marschall, Amy. 2025. "5 TV and movie characters that illustrate anxious attach-ment." Very Well Mind. https://www.verywellmind.com/tv-and-movie-charac ters-with-anxious-attachment-8783608?utm_source=chatgpt.com#toc-donkey-in-shrek.

McGrath, Patrick. 2024. "The ultimate guide to relationship anxiety—and how to overcome it." NOCD Inc. https://www.treatmyocd.com/blog/relationship-anxi ety#h-what-is-relationship-anxiety.

Mindful Health Solutions. 2024. "How to balance your independence and interde-pendence for healthy relationships." https://mindfulhealthsolutions.com/how-to-balance-your-independence-and-interdependence-for-healthy-relationships/.

Moore, Abby. June 20, 2023. "Anxious Attachment: What It Is, Causes, Signs & How To Heal." Mindbodygreen. Accessed March 31, 2025. https://www.mind bodygreen.com/articles/anxious-attachment-style.

Moore, Catherine. 2019. "How to practice self-compassion: 8 techniques and tips." Positive Psychology. https://positivepsychology.com/how-to-practice-self-compas sion/.

O'Bryan, Amanda. 2022. "How to practice active listening: 16 examples & tech-niques." Positive Psychology. https://positivepsychology.com/active-listening-techniques/#what-is-active-listening-3-principles.

Purdue Global. 2024. "What is a growth mindset and how can you develop one?" https://www.purdueglobal.edu/blog/careers/develop-growth-mindset/.

Rao, Gundugurti P., et al. 2024. "Developing resilience and harnessing emotional intelligence." Indian Journal of Psychiatry. https://pmc.ncbi.nlm.nih.gov/arti cles/PMC10911335/.

Raypole, Crystal. 2024. "How to handle relationship anxiety." Healthline. https:// www.healthline.com/health/relationship-anxiety.

Reid, Sheldon. 2025. "Setting healthy boundaries in relationships." HelpGuide.org. https://www.helpguide.org/relationships/social-connection/setting-healthy-boundaries-in-relationships.

Relationships Australia. n.d. "Setting healthy boundaries." https://www.relationship swa.org.au/Tip-sheets/Setting-Healthy-Boundaries.

Robinson, Lawrence, Melinda Smith, and Jeanne Segal. 2024. "Emotional and psychological trauma." HelpGuide.org. https://www.helpguide.org/mental-health/ptsd-trauma/coping-with-emotional-and-psychological-trauma.

Rolston, Abigail, and Elizabeth Lloyd-Richardson. n.d. "What is emotional regulation and how do we do it?" Cornell Research Program on Self-Injury and Recovery. https://selfinjury.bctr.cornell.edu/perch/resources/what-is-emotion-regulationsinfo-brief.pdf.

Sanok, Joe. 2022. "A guide to setting better boundaries." Harvard Business School Publishing. https://hbr.org/2022/04/a-guide-to-setting-better-boundaries.

Schuldt, Woody. n.d. "Grounding techniques." Therapist Aid. https://www.therapistaid.com/therapy-article/grounding-techniques-article.

Sivakumar, Seethalakshmi. 2025. "Sustaining transformation: Techniques for maintaining long-term change." Emocare. https://emocare.co.in/sustaining-transformation-techniques-for-maintaining-long-term-change/.

Stanborough, Rebecca Joy. 2023. "How to change negative thinking with cognitive restructuring." Healthline. https://www.healthline.com/health/cognitive-restructuring#how-does-it-work.

Strand, Paul S et al. 2019. "Culture and child attachment patterns: A behavioral systems synthesis." Perspectives on Behavior Science 42(4): 835-850. https://pubmed.ncbi.nlm.nih.gov/31976462/.

The Attachment Project. 2020. "Anxious attachment: Causes & symptoms." https://www.attachmentproject.com/blog/anxious-attachment/.

The Happy Marriage. 2025. "How to have a hard conversation." https://www.thehappymarriage.com.au/blog/how-to-have-hard-conversations?

Trammell, Crystal. 2024. "Signs of secure attachment: 7 tips to develop a secure attachment." Living Openhearted. https://www.livingopenhearted.com/post/how-to-become-securely-attached.

About the Author

Rochelle Clark, LMT, CLT, is a licensed massage therapist, certified lymphatic therapist, and founder of The Art of Healing Touch, with over 25 years of experience specializing in lymphatic health, breast health, and women's wellness. In Anxious Attachment Recovery Simplified, she shares  practical tools and heartfelt guidance to help readers overcome fear of rejection and reconnect with their authentic selves, while in her spare time she enjoys nature, animals, Pilates, spending time with her family, and curling up with a good book.

Follow Me on Social

Stay Connected https://rochelleclarkbooks.com/contact

Sign up and to receive the latest book releases, special projects, and exclusive tools designed to support your journey—whether you're working on anxious attachment recovery, building self-worth, or deepening your relationships.

You'll also have the unique opportunity to become an Advance Reader Copy reader, getting early access to upcoming books and sharing your valuable feedback.

Plus, you'll receive helpful worksheets, reflection prompts, and wellness resources delivered straight to your inbox. ***Join me and nurture your path to empowered living.***

www.ingramcontent.com/pod-product-compliance
Lightning Source LLC
Chambersburg PA
CBHW030534130626
46552CB00006B/2257